TREASURE THE TRUTH

EMILY SNOW

TREASURE THE TRUTH

Favorite Talks from

ESPECIALLY FOR YOUTH

ACADEMY FOR GIRLS

BOYS WORLD OF ADVENTURE

Covenant Communications, Inc.

Covenant

Published by Covenant Communications, Inc.
American Fork, Utah

Printed in the United States of America
First Printing: April 1997

04 03 02 01 00 99 98 97 10 9 8 7 6 5 4 3 2 1
ISBN 1-57734-120-1

961015-10

Contents

TREASURE THE TRUTH

1

Stripling Saints: Building on the Legacy

Scott Anderson

It was probably a very warm day. Tension filled the air. The drumming sounds of war echoed through the surrounding hills. Today would be unforgettable! Before night came, many would give their lives for their beliefs. Imagine these men hugging their children for one last time. Can you picture families having family prayer together before their loved ones left for the battlefield? How many tears were shed? Why would it end so soon? They had just so recently come to know the joy the gospel brings. But now it was time to go. They left the city and stepped out onto the plains that would soon be stained by their life's blood. Quietly and peacefully, they knelt to pray as oncoming masses, armed and angry, approached. The people were prepared for this day of days.

Not long before this day, neighbors had shouted across the fence, "Hurry to the palace! The king and queen and all their servants are unconscious." Everyone had clamored to see the strange sight. Suddenly, they saw him—a Nephite—among the fallen leaders. Chaos broke out; this Nephite might be the cause of the king and queen's collapse. Perhaps it was a curse. Suddenly, with his sword drawn, a man rushed forward to kill the Nephite; but as he raised his sword he crashed to the floor, dead from the attempt. As the fallen sword's echo silenced, a hush fell over the startled crowd. They may not have noticed Abish, the king's servant, as she took the queen's hand; but they most certainly marveled when the queen arose and revived King Lamoni.

An atmosphere of reverent awe prevailed as the king began to speak, tearfully proclaiming, "I have seen my Redeemer." Then the Nephite Ammon began to teach them the great plan of happiness. These Lamanites felt so much love and peace from the spirit of testimony that they became willing to do anything, to pay any price, to make any sacrifice to keep this joyous brightness of hope resounding in their hearts.

Recalling the gloomy darkness of their feelings in the midst of war and hatred, together with their great desire to never again be estranged from the Spirit, had caused them to prepare for this battle in a most unbelievable way. They had unearthed a veritable chasm in the earth, and had entombed their weapons—swords, cimeters, and their hatred too—and buried them forever, that their swords and lives might never be stained again. (See Alma 24:17-19.)

And so the day arrived. Armed with the peaceful assurance of faithful and humble preparation, the Lamanites stepped onto the plain and stood their tallest as they quietly knelt to pray.

Can we imagine, as the slaughter began, hundreds being massacred without resistance? A literal bloodbath must have washed over the oncoming soldiers as they relentlessly butchered their way forward, repeatedly hearing the peaceful, faith-filled prayers of their Lamanite brothers. How long could such killing continue without opposition? (See Alma 24:21-23.)

After 1,005 had been slain, these assailants finally threw down their swords, crying out with questions such as, "Why? Why are you doing this? Where did you find such a cause for which you would give your lives?" And there in the field, surrounded by the lifeless bodies of their dead relatives and friends, the faithful who survived had another challenge. Could they accept these men—so recently their mortal enemies—as their brothers in the gospel? Looking into the eyes of the men soaked in their neighbors' blood, the remaining faithful began to teach the gospel of love to those who had sought their lives.

More were converted than were slain. (See Alma 24:26.) But what of the families and friends of the 1,005 dead? What was it like for the wives and children who knelt that night without their husbands and fathers?

How many times must the story of this remarkable battle have been shared in the years to follow? How deeply emblazoned in the hearts of the survivors and descendants was the sacred commitment of these men to their covenants. Oh, the lessons their mothers must have taught them! You can almost hear their mothers saying, "You need not fear! Your father didn't fear; you can face your greatest challenges with faith and peace. You need not fear!"

Years later, the battles had become so terrible between the righteous and the wicked that the resources of the faithful were almost spent. Lamoni and his people, who had joined with the Nephites, had kept their covenant not to fight; but the conditions were now so critical that they were about to break it. (See Alma 53:14.) Finally, the prophet Helaman was able to persuade them to keep their covenant.

Then it happened—another day of days. The youth, these children whose forefathers had given their lives for the truth, gathered "themselves" together (Alma 53:16). No one called them to arms; they simply stepped forward—active volunteers! And who did these great youth choose to be their leader—some local hero? No; they chose the prophet. They actively volunteered to follow the prophet Helaman. So, like their fathers, they too entered into a covenant of sacrifice. They would fight to defend their loved ones. (See Alma 53:17.) They were young, valiant for courage, strength, and activity, and true to their duty and the commandments of God. They would face the largest army of the Lamanites (Alma 56:34) without fear, and they would fight with the power of righteousness on their side. Never were men known to have fought with such miraculous strength (Alma 56:56), and none were lost. Helaman called these stripling warriors his sons, for they were really sons of the God whom he served. They had been reared in faith, and were true and sober at all times—real men in the army of God.

How could those 1,005 valiant men who gave their lives have

known that their faithful sacrifice would be a catalyst for incredible courage, binding the hearts of the children to their fathers? Could they have imagined that their own descendants would be the very instruments in the Lord's hands to save a nation? Their legacy of love had flowed from generation to generation, and it still goes on today. President Ezra Taft Benson has stated that "In the spiritual battles you are waging, I see you as today's sons of Helaman" (*Ensign*, May 1986, p. 43). Modern stripling warriors. What a heritage! How has this legacy unfolded in our day?

I don't know if we can even imagine. Perhaps if we really tried . . .

It was frightfully cold on that day in 1856. The snow was so deep on the ground that walking had become almost impossible, and the wind blew the icy crystals into every opening, drifting the camp into a world of white sepulchers. The wagons were no help, and the tents offered little protection as mothers cuddled and rubbed their crying, suffering little ones, trying to create some circulation in their freezing limbs. Weeping was heard, as was the case every morning as a few half-frozen men gathered the dead once again in a now-familiar ritual. Little bodies frozen blue, older men, ashen-faced—all gathered to a shallow opening in the snow, excavated with the meager energy of those who knew it might be their tomb tomorrow. What was it like for a father to carry his lifeless little child to the snow-covered site, knowing the wolves would follow? What of the little boy stumbling from his makeshift tent, leaving a trail of blood in the snow from his frozen feet? He was followed by his little brother of about six years, helping him because he could not walk. They meekly approached a man in camp and begged, "Could you help us? Our parents are both dead in our tent, and we don't know what to do."

How had they prepared to make such sacrifices? Was it the knock of a missionary named Parley upon their door? Was it the invitation in Kirtland to an open meeting to hear the American prophet speak, and as they listened, had they felt so stirred? Was it those who had gone before them on this trail, driven from Nauvoo in the February cold of 1846 onto these plains of sacrifice, who had planted in this very soil the perseverance of faith? Perhaps these handcart families shared the strength that repeatedly came from the well-loved song written from the heartfelt feelings of a father on the plains. In 1846, William Clayton was so many miles away from his wife; she was expecting, and had stayed in Nauvoo. A messenger arrived in camp and informed William that his wife had given birth to a son. The boy was fine, but his wife could die. The message was several days old; might his wife be dead, even now? And what of his son in this largely deserted city? Oh, the emptiness in his heart as he retired to his quiet corner of camp. By morning, young William had penned his deepest feelings in a few tender verses. This prayerful night's quiet answer would bless the Saints for generations to come. It began, "Come, come, ye Saints, no toil nor labor fear; But with joy wend your way." There it was, that message again: You need not fear! No matter what sacrifice you are called on to make, you can face your greatest challenges with faith. You need not fear! Then William went on: "Though hard to you this journey may appear, Grace shall be as your day." Grace—if you do all you can, then the Savior will make up the difference. His sweet influence will help you through the toughest times, just as surely as the sun comes up in the morning, as your day, every day. William also penned a faithful reminder: "And should we die before our journey's through, Happy day! All is well! We then are free from toil and sorrow, too; With the just we shall dwell!" Oh, the strength that said, "Not my will, but thy will." How much faith does it take to be willing to make such a sacrifice? Could these faith-filled words from the husband of a desperately ill wife have comforted this group on the plains as they had so many times before?

Even after the rescue of these suffering and dying pioneers, the consequences continued. At the first farmhouse, Nellie, age ten, was laid upon the kitchen table and her shoes and stockings removed. Her little legs, frozen and poisoned, had to be amputated just below the knees; the carpenter's saw and knife would be used without anything to deaden the pain. She would later raise six children in Deseret, the dirt floor of her home pounded smooth by her knees. She is reported to have observed that the best way to raise children is on one's knees.

Even years later, at a church meeting, a faithless, uninformed man began to criticize the leaders of the Church because of the suffering of the pioneer Saints. Here's what happened:

> An old man in the corner . . . sat silently and listened as long as he could stand it, then he arose and said things that no person who heard him will ever forget. His face was white with emotion, yet he spoke calmly, deliberately, but with great earnestness and sincerity.
>
> In substance [he] said, "I ask you to stop this criticism. You are discussing a matter you know nothing about. Cold historic facts mean nothing here, for they give no proper interpretation of the questions involved. Mistake to send the Handcart Company out so late in the season? Yes. But I was in that company and my wife was in it and Sister Nellie Unthank whom you have cited was there, too. We suffered beyond anything you can imagine and many died of exposure and starvation, but did you ever hear a survivor of that company utter a word of criticism? *Not one of that company ever apostatized or left the Church, because every one of us came through with the absolute knowledge that God lives, for we became acquainted with him in our extremities.*
>
> "I have pulled my handcart when I was so weak and weary from illness and lack of food that I could hardly put one foot ahead of the other. I have looked ahead and seen a patch of sand or a hill slope and I have said, 'I can go only that far and there I must give up, for I cannot pull the load through it.'" He continued, "I have gone on to that sand and when I reached it, the cart began pushing me. I have looked back many times to see who was pushing my cart, but my eyes saw no one. I knew then that the angels of God were there.
>
> "Was I sorry that I chose to come by handcart? No. Neither then nor any minute of my life since. *The price we paid to become acquainted with God was a privilege to pay, and I am thankful that I was privileged to come in the Martin Handcart Company." (Relief Society Magazine,* January 1948, p. 8.)

Why so much sacrifice? Could they have known that hundreds of thousands of their descendants would hear of their legacy of love on the plains of sacrifice and have deeply emblazoned into their hearts a love and appreciation for the faith of their fathers that sustained them? No wonder President Ezra Taft Benson proclaimed, "You are the royal army of the Lord" (*Ensign*, May 1986, p. 43).

The strains still ring from the pioneer camps to our day: "No toil nor labor fear!" You need not fear. Today, our stripling Saints have the enormous task of facing a war of wickedness like we have never seen. You marvelous youth must make the decision to choose a prophet of God as your leader—not some national figure, not some other hero, but the prophet as he represents the Lord. He, too, has called you his sons and daughters.

We see the courage of the great youth of today and feel humbled as you fearlessly face your challenges. Not long ago, we were attending the funeral of a great friend, the mother of six children. She had been active in her community, and had been serving in the stake Young Women's presidency. Cancer had taken this beautiful life so early, and the hall was filled to overflowing with hundreds who had known her. Everyone seemed to think of her as their "best friend," and she was. With all the praise that could have been given her, the special tribute that followed was unforgettable. It was announced that her children would be the principal speakers at the funeral service. The first to stand was a fine young man still in elementary school. He squared his shoulders and in a clear voice said, "I want to share with you a scripture that my mother taught me: ' . . . yet they did not fear . . . they had been taught by their mothers, that if they did not doubt, God would deliver them. And they rehearsed unto me the words of their mothers, saying: We do not doubt our mothers knew it.'" (Alma 56:47-48) Then he quietly but firmly proclaimed, "And I don't fear the future because my mother taught me what I should do."

Speaking to a group of institute of religion teachers one morning, two dedicated, committed young Italian men came to share their testimonies. They were brothers, and had been members of the Church for about eight months. They had both left very good careers and had come to Provo, Utah, to receive more college training and to serve their Heavenly Father. They had given up a great deal, but in their minds had received so much more. As they spoke to us, they recited stories of the pioneers and wept as they talked of their spiritual heritage. They didn't have any pioneer ancestors of their own; not one of their own forefathers had crossed the plains. However, they felt deeply the spiritual heritage that was theirs from the new legacy of faith that was now so personal to them. The truth to them was that their "brothers and sisters" in the gospel had paid this great price for them, and it was now their heritage, too. Each of us can follow this example. These pioneers were our literal brothers and sisters, whether or not we came directly through their bloodlines.

We have a marvelous prophet who stands at the head of the Church today. When being presented to the media as the new president of the Church, President Hinckley proclaimed, "We are particularly proud of our youth. I think we've never had a stronger generation of young men and young women than we have today. For the most part, they are true to the faith of their forebears." When a television reporter from Salt Lake City asked President Hinckley if he would champion a theme during his administration, he replied, "Carry On! Yes. Our theme will be to carry on the great work which has been furthered by our predecessors who have served so admirably, so faithfully, and so well." (Report of the announcement of the new First Presidency, March 13, 1995, Salt Lake City.) On many occasions he has stated, "I have no fear of the future, we have such marvelous youth, facing great challenges yet so faithful and strong." He has repeated this message enough that I have wondered if he sleeps in a "NO FEAR" T-shirt! He calls to us clearly to find our strength in being faith-filled and positive about this great work of the Lord that is before us. Speaking at a fireside in St. George where more than ten thousand youth lined up hours in advance to hear him, President Hinckley said, "Your opportunities are so tremendous, so wonderful. You've come on the scene of the world in the greatest age in the history of mankind. Nobody else has had quite the advantages you have." Then he went on to conclude, "Don't you ever forget, my dear young friends . . . that each of you is a child of God and that your Father in Heaven expects great things of you. . . . I hope you will remember this, that Brother Hinckley told you that you can do it!" (Transcript of an address given by President Hinckley in St. George, Utah, February 1996.)

I know that as you—the stripling Saints who are our youth today—have the courage to follow our wonderful living prophet, we will be able to face the future without fear. After many years of working with you, I, too, am deeply encouraged and echo President Benson's feelings that you are indeed our stripling warriors spiritually. I rally behind President Gordon B. Hinckley and testify that you are incredible youth. There are so many of you working so hard against great odds. You, too, are young, "exceedingly valiant for courage, and also for strength and activity," and can be "true at all times in whatsoever thing [you are] entrusted" (Alma 53:20).

Our wonderful pioneer forefathers were told that they were privileged to lay a foundation for us to build on (D&C 58:7). It is deeply humbling to realize that their tremendous sacrifices were freely given to help us fulfill their—and our—great dreams. Someday as we meet them, they might ask what we did with the foundation they prepared. May we continually build upon their great lives of covenant and sacrifice, moving forward courageously to become a Zion people.

***Scott Anderson** was born in Salt Lake City, Utah. He and his wife, Angelle, live on a small farm in Bluffdale, Utah. They are the parents of seven children; they also have two grandchildren and one on the way. Scott earned a Ph.D. in marriage and family therapy from Brigham Young University and currently teaches at the Orem Institute adjacent to Utah Valley State College in Orem, Utah. He has taught in the Church Educational System since 1973 in programs such as Academy for Girls, Especially for Youth, Education Week, Education Days, Know Your Religion, and the Women's Enrichment Program.*

2

The Look

Curtis Galke

During my senior year in high school I decided I wanted to be a physician. I was sure no other occupation could be as fun or fulfilling. In surgery I could cut out something harmful that wasn't supposed to be there. I could see myself being called to the Emergency Room to set a broken bone or stop someone from bleeding. However, I could never have imagined that the most rewarding times I would share with people would be those tender hours waiting for death to mercifully take a struggling patient home, and those humbling minutes during which I would have the opportunity to hold a brand new baby in my arms as it took its first breath.

The birth of the Wilcox twins was one of those experiences. Mrs. Wilcox was sent to our hospital in southern Texas by her family doctor in order to evaluate her pregnancy. She was carrying twins that didn't seem to be growing the way they should have been. Ultrasound tests showed that one twin was growing considerably faster than the other, and in a matter of days the smaller twin would not have much chance for survival if we didn't intervene. Our medical plan was to figure out when we could deliver both twins safely. If we delivered too early, both infants would be in danger. If we waited too long, the smaller twin would surely die.

On the morning of the delivery, the operating room was buzzing with doctors and nurses anticipating the birth; everyone in the room had their own assigned responsibility. I listened as monitors beeped and incubators hummed. After several hours of labor the larger twin was born—a beautiful little girl with a great set of lungs! Doctors quickly took her to an incubator and examined her. Everything appeared to be normal and a sense of relief settled over the rest of us in the delivery room.

Anxiously we awaited the delivery of the other twin. We knew his condition would be more guarded. After several more minutes, the physician carefully delivered the tiny little boy. However, something was obviously wrong. The infant was limp, blue, and very small. We would later find out that he weighed only two pounds and four ounces, just a little more than a few sticks of butter.

Another team of doctors and nurses attempted to resuscitate the little boy. All eyes were glued on the incubator, hoping for some movement. No one spoke as we waited to hear the baby's cry. Minutes seemed like hours. Finally a gasp and a weak cry, and the little boy was rushed off to the neonatal intensive care unit.

Hours later, after my work was done for the day, I stopped by the unit to check on the little boy. The consensus among the medical staff was that he didn't have much of a chance. I made my way through the ICU looking for the Wilcox boy. I had never seen so many really sick kids in one place before; it seemed that each was attached to tubes and machines.

When I finally found the twin I was looking for, he was breathing with the help of a ventilator, he had IVs in each arm and his eyes were taped down to protect them from the light in his incubator. I sat there for several minutes looking at him, wondering what chance he had. Life was starting off hard for him. There were so many struggles and hardships to overcome; even the experts said he probably couldn't make it.

As one of the nurses taking care of the Wilcox boy approached the incubator to change the ventilator settings, she noticed me deep in thought.

"Do you have any questions?" the elderly nurse asked me. She appeared to have had plenty of experience working with sick kids over the years so I asked her, "Do you think he'll make it?"

Without any hesitation she said, "Oh he'll make it. He's got the look."

What in the world is "the look?" I wondered. *He looks pretty helpless and fragile to me.*

The nurse continued, "I've seen a lot of babies here; some have made it, others have not." Nodding at the little two-pound boy, she said, "He has the look of a survivor."

In 1830, the Lord told the prophet Joseph Smith, "Be patient in afflictions, for thou shalt have many; but endure them, for, lo, I am with thee, even unto the end of thy days" (D&C 24:8). The Lord has promised that afflictions or challenges will come to all of us. He knows our strengths and weaknesses, and has tailored experiences in this life for us that develop our weaknesses into strengths (see Ether 12:27). All too often we compare our trials to the trials of others and wonder why we got the heavier load. We complain that life just isn't fair.

But our challenges are unique to us, given to us to develop our individual strengths and weaknesses. Since affliction and hard times will come to us all, we need to develop "the look" which will enable us to endure well the afflictions that the Lord has promised will come our way.

The first step toward developing "the look" is to figure out what our attitude toward trials really is. Do we see them as opportunity or as devastation? When problems come, do we plead for them to be taken away or do we pray for understanding in order to be able to grow? Elder Richard G. Scott reminds us: "It is important to understand that His healing can mean being cured, or having your burdens eased, or even coming to realize that it is worth it to endure to the end patiently, for God needs brave sons and daughters who are willing to be polished when in His wisdom that is His will" (*Ensign*, May 1994, p. 7).

Death, heartache, loneliness, physical illness, pain as well as other problems don't come as a punishment nor as divine rejection. They are simply part of God's plan for our progression. Hardship and trial will come to those who do their best to keep the Lord's commandments as well as to those who do not obey.

Several years ago while reading in the *Church News,* I stumbled onto a headline that not only caught my interest but tugged at my heart. The headline read, "Funeral Replaces Traditional Homecoming," and the article related the story of Elder Gale Stanley Critchfield, who, while serving as a full-time missionary in the Ireland Dublin Mission, was killed when he was stabbed in the heart on the way home from a church meeting. President Hinckley speaking at Elder Critchfield's funeral, said, "This is a day of sadness, a day of wondering. We wonder why, when a young man is called to serve the Lord, he isn't watched over so closely his life is protected. We don't know the purposes of the Lord. We don't know why some things happen. . . ." (*Church News,* June 9, 1990, p. 3). What could Elder Critchfield or his family have possibly done to deserve such an affliction? What a ridiculous question, and yet isn't that the same question we ask ourselves as we wonder "Why me?" when we have our own troubles? In setting apart Elder Critchfield as a missionary, his stake president promised him that "the last night [Elder Critchfield] would spend in the Ireland Dublin Mission, the Savior would come to him and embrace him in His arms and say to him, 'Well done, my faithful son'" (*Church News,* June 9, 1990, p. 4).

Was Elder Critchfield's affliction a devastation or a blessing seldom had by a full-time missionary? It really is a matter of attitude.

The winter of 1838 was a bleak time for the prophet Joseph Smith. The prophet had been betrayed and thrown into the Liberty jail with several other Church leaders without cause. For five months those men were called upon to endure hardships that defy belief. The winter was particularly cold. The jail was small, drafty, and damp. There was no bathroom or shower. They were given little food, and at times it was laced with poison. There was nowhere to sleep but on beds made of straw, placed on hard wood and stone floors. During those months in Liberty Jail, the prophet asked the Lord about his afflictions. The Lord answered, "My son, peace be unto thy soul; thine adversity and thine afflictions shall be but *a small moment*; and then if thou endure it *well,* God shall exalt thee on high" (D&C 121:7-8; emphasis added).

If you read that with your spiritual eyes, you learned two important truths about trials. The first is that in the eternal scheme of things, no matter how hard and long our challenges may seem to us, even if they last a lifetime, in reality they are but a small moment. Second, we must not only endure (do we really have any other choice?), but we must endure our afflictions *well.*

Perhaps one of the greatest examples of enduring afflictions well was the prophet Abinadi in the Book of Mormon. Having been sent to a formerly righteous but now rebellious people, he worked day and night to complete the assignment the Lord had given him. Though he was obedient, affliction and hardship followed him the whole time he worked with the people of King Noah. Abinadi did all he was asked to do, but he was put in prison, beaten, and eventually was thrown out of the city. Abinadi didn't wander around in the jungle depressed wondering why the Lord had asked so much of him and given apparently so little in return. After all he had sacrificed to the cause in which the Lord had enlisted him, he had no converts, no followers, and, it surely must have seemed to him, no visible measure of success. As he stood in the middle of the flames that would take his life he didn't ask, "Why me, Lord? I've done all that thou hast asked." Rather he continued to do the work he was called to do as he testified and taught with his dying breath.

In order to deal well with our trials and afflictions, we must put them in the proper perspective as tools that a loving Father uses to teach and train his children in their quest to become like him.

> No pain that we suffer, no trial that we experience is wasted. It ministers to our education, to the development of such qualities as patience, faith, fortitude, and humility. All that we suffer and all that we endure, especially when we endure it patiently, builds up our characters, purifies our hearts, expands our souls, and makes us more tender and charitable, and more worthy to be called the children of God . . . and it is through sorrow and suffering, toil and tribulation, that we gain the education that we came here to acquire and which will make us more like our Father . . . in heaven (Orson F.

Whitney as quoted in *Faith Precedes the Miracle*, Spencer W. Kimball, p. 98).

The second step in getting "the look" and enduring our trials well is illustrated by Alma, who unknown to Abinadi, had not only heard but responded to the prophet's message. While teaching in a particularly wicked city, Alma and his missionary companion, Amulek, had plenty of trials and afflictions of their own. The rulers of the city of Ammonihah burned those who accepted the teaching of the missionaries and put Alma and Amulek into prison. While imprisoned Alma and Amulek were deprived of food and water, stripped of their clothing, and tied up with "strong cords." Alma 14 tells us that for many days the rulers would visit Alma and Amulek in jail repeatedly mocking them, hitting them, and spitting on them. Alma's response to his hardships teaches us a great lesson: "*How long* shall we suffer these great afflictions, O Lord? O Lord, give us strength according to our *faith* which is in Christ" (Alma 14:26; emphasis added).

Although I had memorized Alma 32:21 and Hebrews 11:1 in seminary, I don't think I really understood what faith was until I was riding a bus through the Mexican countryside as a missionary. It was in the spring of the year, and for miles I watched as poor peasant farmers were tilling the ground and preparing the soil. They worked with old broken tools and sickly looking mules in order to get their crop of corn planted. After their work of preparation was over, I watched as they went through the tedious and physically demanding work of planting the seeds one by one. They would take a seed out of a bag, bend over, place it in the ground, then cover it up, moving ever so slowly down the row. Since these people had little money, buying seeds was quite an investment and I couldn't help but think of how ironic it was that they would take their investment and bury it in the ground with only the hope of a future harvest. These people were not great scientists who understood botany, photosynthesis, and the biochemistry by which plants grow. Yet week after week, those faithful farmers were in the fields, hoeing, weeding, watering, and fertilizing, all the while hoping that the seeds would sprout, grow, develop, and produce a harvest.

Faith is hope that is powerful enough to motivate us to work—even in the absence of a complete understanding of how things will eventually turn out. As members of the Church we believe that our Heavenly Father and his Son live, that they love us, and that if we are faithful to the end, we will return home to them. When that belief is strong enough to motivate us to go to church, attend seminary, fill honorable full-time missions, marry in the temple, and do our best to obey the commandments, we are exercising faith. Yet even when motivated to live a good life, the Lord has promised us that afflictions and trouble will come just as they came to the Savior, Abinadi, Alma, and Joseph Smith. The survivor's "look" comes as we put our complete trust in his purposes even in those darkest hours.

I became friends with a young boy who had "the look" several months before I finished my mission. I met Oscar when my companion and I went to the hospital to give him a blessing. He had been diagnosed with a rare cancer. We arrived at the hospital and Oscar not knowing me, but recognizing the white shirt and tie of a missionary grabbed my finger and led me into the room of his friend who was about to lose a leg to an infection. Oscar had explained to his friend that the missionaries would be visiting and could give him a blessing to heal his leg. Oscar looked up at me and said, "Elder, give him the blessing!" Humbled by his faith, my companion and I gave his friend a blessing. As a matter of fact we gave blessings to many of his friends that day.

Oscar turned eight years old several weeks after I met him. His dream was to be the first one baptized in the new building his ward was constructing. As we would with any other investigator, my companion and I taught him the discussions, or should I say he taught them to us! The entire ward attended this inaugural baptism in their new building. As I watched Oscar come up out of the water, he seemed to glow. Seldom have I seen anyone who was as excited about his membership in the Lord's church. The next Sunday in testimony meeting, after expressing gratitude for his membership in the church, Oscar announced his plans to serve a full-time mission and enlisted the help of the members in building up his missionary savings fund. Oscar suffered a great deal of pain and humiliation with his cancer. He lost all of his hair and was often quite sick. He was in and out of the hospital several times in the next few months.

On one of the more painful days, a priest came to visit, stating that he would like to pray for the little boy who appeared to be dying. At hearing that, Oscar sat up and said to the priest, "I am a member of The Church of Jesus Christ of Latter-day Saints. I am not going to die. I am going to serve a mission for my church." Oscar then related the Joseph Smith story after which he invited the stunned priest to attend church with him.

Over the six months I knew Oscar, we grew very close. A week before I returned home, I went to the hospital one last time to visit with Oscar and to tell him that my mission was over. It was a tender time for me. Three days later, the bishop of the ward called to tell me that Oscar had slipped into a coma and wasn't expected to live. We got to the hospital late at night, and for the next several hours I sat at Oscar's side. I thought about him, his trials and his faith, and I came to realize that bad things can happen to good people, but that when they do, there is a wise purpose and our Father is never far away. I know that is true. I felt Him there that night. Early that morning Oscar left on his mission. Many years have past since I said good-bye to my friend, but I'll never forget "the look" he had.

As we face our trials with the right attitude and perspective, trusting completely in our Father and his purposes, I testify that we will have "the look" and be able to bear well our afflictions. For the Lord has said, "Be patient in afflictions, for thou shalt have many; but endure them [well], for, lo, I am with thee, even unto the end of thy days" (D&C 24:8).

Curtis Galke *served a mission in Mexico City and later taught Spanish and Ambassadorship at the Missionary Training Center. After graduating from Brigham Young University, he attended medical school in California. Curtis completed a three-year residency in family practice with the U.S. Air Force, and then was sent to the Republic of Panama to fill his military commitment. Currently Curtis is a faculty member in a family practice residency program in southern Illinois. Curtis and his wife, Alethea, have three active sons.*

3

"The Greatest in the Kingdom of Heaven"

Steven T. Linford

"We've got problems," said my wife, Melanie, as I walked in the door after a day of teaching seminary. "Tell me about it," I replied. "No really," she continued. "You need to go talk to your oldest son. He is in his room." My oldest son is named C.J., and at the time he was six years old. I walked to C.J.'s room. "Hi, C.J." I said. "Oh, hi, Dad," he responded. "I understand you had a problem today." A big smile came over C.J.'s face. He looked at me and while grinning he said, "Dad, I like girls." I said, "You what?" C.J. looked at me and repeated again, "Dad, I like girls." I said, "C.J., what about basketball?" (I'm raising my sons to be basketball men.) "Dad, I don't like basketball any more. I like girls," he said. I said, "Oh C.J., yuck!" C.J. looked at me and said, "No dad, yummm!" The rest of the night each time I looked at C.J., I would point at him and say, "Basketball." He would smile and point back at me and say, "Girls."

Almost daily this same son will say things that make me laugh. Last year, a week before his baptism, he said to me, "Now, Dad, when you put me under the water, don't leave me under very long. You see, I can't breathe there very well." I promised him that I would "put him under" for just a short time.

Little children are great! They are a constant source of joy and happiness. My wife and I currently have three. I love being around them, listening to them, and playing with them. They have a certain innocence, a certain purity.

Last fall my family and I went to the open house of the Mount Timpanogos Temple. It was a rainy day and we were grateful to enter the sheltered area to wait our turn to tour the temple. As we came in from the rain, we were met by a small choir of Hispanic children who were happily singing Primary songs in Spanish. This was a treat to all of us, but especially for our children. We toured the beautiful temple, keeping a quick pace as we unsuccessfully tried to keep up with Kolby, our two-year-old son. We were in awe of the splendid spirit and magnificent beauty of this sacred building. Soon we exited the temple and began making our way to the car. It was raining hard, and we could hear the "rolling thunder" as well as see the lightning. Finally, we reached the car and entered into its comfort. As I started the car, we looked at the exterior of this lovely temple, and C.J. said, "Dad, somebody better tell Angel Moroni to get off the temple before he gets hit by lightning!"

On one occasion the disciples came to the Savior, and asked, "Who is the greatest in the kingdom of heaven?" Jesus responded by calling a little child unto him, then setting the little boy in their midst said, "Verily I say unto you, Except ye be converted, and become as little children, ye shall not enter into the kingdom of heaven" (Matthew 18:1-4).

Now, it is important to realize that there is a big difference between becoming like a little child or child*like*, and becoming like a little brat, or child*ish*. Jesus wants us to become the former, not the latter. He was referring to the humble selfless qualities of children, not the defiant, selfish behaviors.

It is interesting to note that becoming child*like* is similar to becoming Christ*like*. The qualities are similar. We see in Jesus as well as children the extraordinary ability to love people, to forgive people, to care for people. Those who are childlike are humble; they are submissive or, in other words, they are teachable.

In Mosiah 3:19 we read, "For the natural man is an enemy to

God, and has been from the fall of Adam, and will be, forever and ever, unless he yields to the enticings of the Holy Spirit, and putteth off the natural man and becometh a saint through the atonement of Christ the Lord, *and becometh as a little child,* submissive, meek, humble, patient, full of love, willing to submit to all things which the Lord seeth fit to inflict upon him, even as a child doth submit to his father."

I have often seen the quality of humility, a reverence for the sacred, displayed in children. Earlier this year, just two days before Halloween, my family and I were sitting at our kitchen table, drawing faces on and carving pumpkins. My little daughter, Kilee, looked at her mother and said, "Mom, I don't want to dress up as a bride for Halloween any more." My wife raised her eyebrows and answered, "Well, we already have the dress, the veil and the bouquet of flowers, but you can be something else if you want. What would you like to be instead?"

Kilee paused and then answered, "I want to be one of those nice boys that brings us the bread and water on Sunday." I caught my wife's eye as she and I began to chuckle. "Oh," my wife said, "you want to be a deacon for Halloween." Kilee smiled broadly, revealing her missing two front teeth. "Yes," she agreed. "I want to be a deacon for Halloween . . . and . . . maybe I could get a plate and put pieces of bread and little cups of water on it and carry it with me when I go trick-or-treating. Pleeeaase, can I please be a deacon, Mom?"

Trying not to laugh, my wife said, "It would probably be better if you weren't a deacon for Halloween. Why don't you choose something else?" As Kilee stared at the pumpkin on which she had just drawn a friendly pumpkin face, I could tell her mind was searching for something that she considered important. Finally, she exclaimed, "Then I want to be a missionary for Halloween! I'll borrow C.J.'s suit and tie, and we could find an old missionary tag for me. I can even carry a Book of Mormon as I go trick-or-treating. Pleeeaase, can I please be a missionary, Mom?"

Well, up to that point I had been sitting there enjoying the whole conversation. Then my wife said, "Ask your father, Kilee, and if he says it's okay, then it's okay with me, and you can be a missionary for

Halloween." Turning her big blue eyes toward me, Kilee pleaded, "Can I, Dad, can I?" "Kilee," I said, thinking I could talk her out of it. "Don't you have to wear your costume to school that day?" "Yes," she answered. "And you still want to be a missionary?" Her answer was definite: "Yes, Dad, I do!" "Well, okay," I said. "If you want to be a missionary for Halloween, that's fine with me."

Sure enough Kilee dressed up as a missionary that day and night, and made the cutest-looking missionary trick-or-treater I've ever seen.

Jesus also said, "Whosoever therefore shall humble himself as this little child, the same is greatest in the kingdom of heaven" (Matt. 18:4).

How humble are we? Are we as humble as a little child? It's often helpful to evaluate our own level of humility by asking ourselves a few questions such as the following:

1. Do we regard the things of the Spirit with reverence and sacredness?

2. Are we willing to serve God at any time, under any circumstance?

3. Do we selflessly serve others without expecting anything in return, including personal or public recognition?

4. Do we "cry unto the Lord in mighty prayer," recognizing our complete dependence on our Father?

5. Do we realize that the only way back to our Heavenly Father is through the atonement of Jesus Christ?

Questions like these can serve as an important reminder about the need for humility. Remember, he or she who "shall humble himself as [a] little child, the same is greatest in the kingdom of heaven."

In the Book of Mormon we read, "Therefore, whoso repenteth and cometh unto me as a little child, him will I receive, for of such is the kingdom of God. Behold, for such I have laid down my life, and have taken it up again; therefore repent, and come unto me ye ends of the earth, and be saved" (3 Nephi 9:22).

This verse not only illustrates the need of repentance, but also demonstrates the attitude that is found in little children. In the phrase ". . . *cometh unto me as a little child, him will I receive. . .*," we see that there is something in the attitude of a little child that makes him or her acceptable to the Lord. When we are childlike, we are easily corrected, easily taught, submissive, and forgiving.

Being a dad I've learned that sometimes I have to correct my children. One night while I was at home with my family, the doorbell rang. I started to the door to answer it, but my son ran past me. "I'll get it," he said. When he reached the door, he turned the knob, opened it, and looked at our visitors. "Oh no," he said, "not you again! I don't like you any more!" and he slammed the door. Horrified, I quickly reopened the door, and much to my embarrassment I saw our home teachers standing there. I apologized and invited them into our home, and they gave our family a nice lesson. They've always structured their lessons to meet the ages of my children, and after the lesson, we thanked our home teachers and they said goodbye. As I closed the door, I turned to look at my son. He looked at me, hung his head, and said, "I go sit on my bed now." "Yes," I said, "you go sit on your bed now."

After a while, I entered my son's room. He was sitting on his bed with a sullen look on his face. We sat and talked and after a while he gave me a hug and said softly, "Sorry, Daddy."

We all make mistakes. But sometimes we resent being corrected; we defiantly reject authority and rebelliously defend our actions. But as I look back on the experience of my son with the home teachers, I hope that I would have the same attitude as a little child when I make mistakes.

Another quality I have seen in little children is their desire to learn about Heavenly Father and Jesus. Last spring we decided to take our children to Disneyland. A few rows ahead of us on the plane sat a little boy and a little girl. After approximately thirty minutes in the air, the little boy said in a voice loud enough for all to hear, "Mom, we've been in the air a long time now, and I haven't seen Heavenly Father or Jesus yet." Apparently this little boy knew that Heavenly Father and Jesus lived in heaven, and he thought that he would have a chance to see them while we were flying in the sky!

To give another example, a few years ago my little daughter and I went on a mountain walk. She had a question from our family home evening lesson she wanted to ask me about. "You know how you said that when we die our bodies go in the ground," she said. "Well something is bothering me." "What is it?" I asked. This was her question: "Dad, when we die, how will we see? If our bodies are in the ground, and our eyeballs are in our bodies, then how will we see when we die?" I couldn't think of how to answer, so I just said, "Kilee, why don't you ask your mom this question? She can help you with the answer."

I love to read about the beautiful experience of the Master, Jesus Christ, when he visits the Nephites (see 3 Nephi 17). He allows the multitude to feel the prints of the nails in his hands and in his feet, he calls and commissions the twelve disciples, and then he teaches them a wonderful sermon. When Jesus announces that he must leave, the people begin to cry and they ask him to stay a little longer. Jesus is filled with compassion, and he stays with them and heals all the people who are lame, blind, halt, maimed, leprous, withered, deaf, or afflicted in any manner. The people gratefully and humbly kneel down at his feet and worship him and bathe his feet with their tears.

Jesus then commands the Nephites to bring all of their little children to him, and after the children are all gathered together, Jesus prays to the Father. This fills everyone with great joy. After the prayer Jesus says, "Blessed are ye because of your faith. And now behold, my joy is full. And when he had said these words, he wept, and the multitude bare record of it, and he took their little children, one by one, and blessed them, and prayed unto the Father for them. And when he had done this he wept again; And he spake unto the multitude, and said unto them: Behold your little ones." At this time the multitude witnessed angels "descending out of heaven as it were in the midst of fire; and they came down and encircled those little ones about, and they were encircled about with fire; and the angels did minister unto them" (verses 20-24).

What a tremendous experience this must have been to the children! To have the knowledge that they had been blessed by the hands of the Savior. This certainly would have had an impact on their entire life. What a tremendous experience this must have been to the parents of the children—to see their children being blessed by Jesus.

We see in this chapter as well as or better than any where else in scripture the feelings the Savior has for children. He loved them, he gathered them near to him, and he blessed them. On another occasion Jesus said, "Suffer little children, and forbid them not, to come unto me: for of such is the kingdom of heaven" (Matthew 19:14). Jesus wants us to become like them, so that he can bless us and protect us.

In my home hangs my favorite picture. The picture illustrates Jesus with little children, his hands gently touching one child's face. This picture is also on my desk at work. It reminds me not only of how Jesus treated little children, but also the statement that "except [we] be converted, and become as little children, [we] shall not enter into the kingdom of heaven" (Matthew 18:3).

It is my fervent hope that we will continually strive to become as little children and that we will be "humble, patient, full of love, willing to submit to all things which the Lord seeth fit to inflict upon him, even as a child doth submit to his father."

Steven T. Linford *has degrees from the University of Utah and Utah State University, and is currently working toward a Ph.D. at Brigham Young University in family studies. He loves to play basketball, run, bike, swim, and spend time with his family. He and his wife, Melanie, reside with their three children in Elk Ridge, Utah, where Steve currently serves as bishop of the Elk Ridge Second Ward.*

4

One by One

Kathy Schlendorf

Every school has one—an adult who effortlessly makes kids feel natural, accepted, and welcome. At my school this pied piper listens to them, nodding intently. He never interrupts or rushes the kids. As they warm to their subject, out comes the bag of chips, which he munches while the kids dump their guts into his lap. Without even realizing they are doing it, the kids shove their fists into the chip bag as he holds it out to them. They chew and talk and relax, and then they open their spirits to his counsel. His words are brief and wise. Usually they are packaged in humor and a relaxed assurance of confidence that he knows the kid can succeed. This is a chat, after all, over a bag of chips, and not a session where the adult sets out to "fix" the kid. Because of his own medley of life challenges, my friend simply understands where these kids are coming from. This quiet hero suggests a gentle solution to the problem offered, and each young person leaves his office with more courage to face what they had found so impossible a few minutes before. This man ministers. One by one.

I spotted him last August when half of the faculty from each of the existing middle schools in Provo joined as the first faculty of the new one. He is not remarkably handsome nor particularly young. It is not his magic on the ball field that attracts the kids, although I suspect he can run about as well as anyone and could throw a mean ball if the occasion required it. All you have to do is talk to this man for three minutes, and you feel the cloak of his humor, his acceptance, and his wisdom begin to wrap around you.

Now this kind of ministering fascinates me, so I kept my eye on him. It didn't take long before I got him talking. I'll call him Jeff. I was amazed and saddened to learn that Jeff is no longer active in the Church. "I'm not particularly religious," he told me honestly. "Not religious at all." It is important to him to be straightforward. I tried not to stare. Somewhere along the line, Jeff lost touch with the Man whose example he unknowingly follows.

How does that happen? How can we lose the reality of the fact that the Savior reaches out to us one by one, touching our lives as individuals?

Do you remember in 3 Nephi when Jesus visits the surviving descendants of Lehi? In chapter 17 the Lord finishes his first day of ministering. He is ready to depart for the day, and he invites the people to "go unto your homes and ponder upon the things which I have said. . . . And . . . when Jesus had thus spoken, he cast his eyes round about again on the multitude, and beheld they were in tears, and did look steadfastly upon him as if they would ask him to tarry a little longer with them" (verses 3, 5).

Was he too busy? He had just told them he needed to go to his Father and also to show himself to the lost tribes of Israel (see verse 4). He had appointments. He had a world to run. But when he looked at them, his schedule changed. "My bowels are filled with compassion toward you. Have ye any that are sick among you? Have ye any that are lame, or blind, or halt; or maimed, or leprous, or that are withered, or that are deaf, or that are afflicted in any manner?" (verses 6- 7). He understood the exact condition they were in.

Does he know *me?* Do you ever wonder that? Does he know *my* weaknesses? Does he care about *my* suffering? Does he have compassion for the struggles with which *I* deal?

"And he shall go forth, suffering pains and afflictions and temptations of *every kind;* and this that the word might be fulfilled which saith *he will take upon him* the pains and the sicknesses of his people"

(Alma 7:11; emphasis added).

That same late afternoon, the Savior commanded that the little children should be brought to him (3 Nephi 17:11). He took *each* child *one at a time*—as individuals— "and blessed them and prayed unto the Father for them" (verse 21).

He sends a home teacher quietly into the home to love us, as his messenger. He touches us through a bishop, one at a time in private confidential interviews. I have felt no greater presence of the Lord's individual ministering than behind those gentle bishops' doors.

Somewhere, years ago, as a kid himself, Jeff slipped through the cracks. No one ever took out a bag of chips and listened to him—no one knocked on his door, grabbed him from the TV, or the Nintendo, or the other distractions that can displace the gospel in our lives—and loved him back.

Jeff was *sent* to church as a boy, not taken. He says his mother still does not understand that that was a mistake. His dad was not interested (for whatever reasons gnawed at the dad's heart). We need to stop and understand something right now. Most of us are not basically "evil"—we search for something to hang onto. If we don't find the iron rod, we will accept counterfeits. The back seat of the car does not offer eternal life. But it offers a delicious moment of closeness, of a sensation that makes us feel wanted. We slip into counterfeits because we are hungry for what we do not have. It is so intensely important to reach out to one another and offer the love that the Savior has given to us. We need to arrive home in groups. It is hard to get there alone.

When Jeff hit his teenage years, he eagerly joined his dad and his older brothers in their Sunday ritual of motorcycling. Picture the scene: every week he and his little sister were sent to church while he watched his dad and his two older brothers go off to the desert. Which would you have chosen at age thirteen? Wouldn't he imagine the smell of sagebrush, the warmth of the dirt rising in his nostrils? Could he hear the roar of the engines and smell the gasoline that heralded a day of adventure under a gorgeous blue sky? There is no way a thirteen-year-old kid could resist being included. Do you see why it is so important that parents lead their children to the Lord?

He also started drinking beer when he was fourteen. Only a third of a can at first. The stuff is so awful that it takes time to learn to like it. Part of the ritual included guzzling the bubbly stuff inside the chilled and dripping cans of beer grabbed from the ice-filled cooler strapped on the back of one of the bikes. When you get used to getting buzzed every Sunday afternoon at age fourteen, how do you get a high at age sixteen? Or eighteen? Jeff didn't have a chance.

One day, at the dusky close of one of their male-bonding "beer-commercial" days, Jeff's father rode out to bring everyone back in. The sky was gray, heading into the azure black that precedes night-fall. A car sped along the road, its lights blinding. The second son and the father crashed into each other in a head-on collision that took both of their lives. Jeff sat on his motorcycle and watched it happen. It was over before he could even react.

Where were the ministers to reach out to this kid? Where were the other youth in his quorum? Where were his priesthood leaders? He admits that he didn't want anyone around. He admits that he had sharp quills out to keep everyone away. But is that a good enough excuse? Is it good enough to be scared away because a kid drinks beer? Did Jeff's soul stop being important because he struggled with so much? Who is in your quorum? In your classes at school? On your bus? In your neighborhood?

One day this young man stopped the drugs himself. He put himself through college, got a teaching degree, got a job. He is currently straight as a rainstick, and filled with the same soothing song. This he uses to reach out to kids at our school.

Why do we ignore those around us who need our ministering? Why do we sometimes fail to take upon us the name of the Savior and his example and his work and glory? Is it so hard to imagine that you and I can help "bring to pass the immortality and eternal life of man"? (Moses 1:39). We all waited in line to come to earth together. We all waited a lot of years. Do you believe that? I feel certain that we made friends. That we made promises to each other. "I'll come find you" is the one we hear romanticized the most. Lots of missionaries search for two years to fulfill that specific promise. I am grateful to the missionaries who taught me the gospel, and to the intense friend of mine who cut to the chase and asked me if I knew who Joseph Smith was. Only a few years later Jack Gardener died in Vietnam as a twenty-one-year-old soldier; I may be his only "convert." He had made no excuses as an eighteen-year-old. He simply bit the bullet and ministered to me. The elders visited my house with only me there to teach. I was just a fifteen-year-old kid, not an entire family. Perhaps the elders persisted only because of that romanticized promise to come find me.

I *am* grateful they kept that promise, but there are so many other ways to minister: the words (and the promises) "I will be kind to you," "I will listen to you," "I will drive you to church," "I will befriend you even though you let go of the iron rod" are all equally important. They can each be lifesaving. Without examples of his love, many of us will never believe it exists. And we will cling to our counterfeits.

The Savior prophesied that one day many "will sell me for silver and for gold, and for that which moth doth corrupt, and which thieves can break through and steal" (3 Nephi 27:32). We will be so busy with our distractions that we will forget to be even as the Savior is. He asks us to do those things which we have seen him do (see 3 Nephi 27:21). Ministering one by one is certainly not the least important of the Lord's examples. My daughter learned about humble consistent ministering on her mission. She told me she learned so many things during those intense eighteen months, many of which she did not know she needed to learn.

My Tarisse served in the California Los Angeles Mission, Spanish speaking. She lived with those humble immigrants who have come to this country as visitors, hopeful to be allowed to stay. They speak only their language. They find very menial jobs in factories or as laborers. They have no opportunities to be business owners, doctors, lawyers, teachers, etc. She met wonderfully humble faithful members of the Church who lived in tragic poverty, but who lifted and loved each other. They remembered to minister. One experience she relates took place on an ordinary Tuesday. She and her companion were on bikes (an interesting way to travel the gang-infested streets of the ghettos in east L.A.). They had a large area to cover, and many people to teach. On this particular day they had not eaten at all. They were scurrying from one teaching appointment to another. In many missions this would not be considered a hardship at all! Some elders and sisters rarely get into a home to teach.

Tarisse and her companion had an appointment with Joe Martinez at seven o'clock one evening. He was an older gentleman, in his sixties. He had listened to several discussions, and the two young women were hopeful that he would soon be baptized. They did not stop for supper because they did not want to miss him or make him wait, and they had other appointments after his. It was one of those exhausting days that were so familiar to them.

When they arrived at Joe's humble apartment, a teenage boy opened the door. A homeless youth who lived with Joe, he told the sisters that Joe was gone for a moment but would be right back. The sisters were invited to sit down, and they relished a quiet minute on the couch with nothing to do. When Joe returned, he had a sack in his hand from a fast-food hamburger store. He went into the kitchen and got two plates and put two chicken sandwiches on them. He had also stopped at the store and bought a gallon of milk. He filled two cups and handed those to the sisters also.

The sisters knew Joe's situation. He was employed, but didn't earn enough to live on. For the last two weeks of every month he was without money and usually without much food in the cupboards.

Joe did not have a car. He didn't have money in his budget for the bus or a cab; he walked everywhere he went. That night he had walked over half a mile each way to get those chicken sandwiches for his *hermanitas.* He spent his last money for them. There was no other food in the house. Tarisse knew this. How could she eat this sandwich when it was all Joe had? He sat across from them and smiled happily.

"How did you know we were hungry?" Tarisse asked him. He paused just a moment, and then answered her, "God told me. He told me the sisters had not eaten today and would be hungry." How could she refuse his sandwich now? Nothing had ever tasted so precious to her.

Like that, the Spirit whispers to us one at a time. The Holy Ghost witnesses to us one at a time. The Savior atones for us, one at a time. We repent on our knees one at a time. We find others to serve one at a time. It is a pattern the Savior introduced.

Tarisse tried more than once to give Joe money. He was very hurt by that. But once he did confess that he wished he had scripture tapes so that he could listen while he walked everywhere. It takes time for an older man to walk, and this is what he would choose as a companion if it were possible. He was not hinting. New in the gospel, he was a very simple man. He was simply telling her his wish. She had a box of Spanish Book of Mormon scripture tapes with her on her mission. She wrapped them up and made them a gift before she was released. His eyes misted up. "I will save for headphones and listen as I walk everywhere!" For him the tapes were a gift from God.

What a privilege to be a part of the work of ministering angels. There is so much to be done if we will open our ears and our hearts and listen to the promptings of the Spirit.

Another angel my daughter met while on her mission is Sister Padron. A busy woman, she has a full-time job, four children, a home to care for. She is both a Sunday School and a Relief Society teacher. My daughter told me she also spends hundreds of hours serving the members in her ward. There are new ones arriving all the time—either through the missionaries or newly arrived from another country. Sister Padron seeks them out. She listens to the Spirit. No doubt she kneels every morning and asks Heavenly Father to inspire her to know who needs her that day, and she follows what the Spirit whispers. Sister Padron will walk up to a newly arrived member and ask, "How are you?"

"I'm fine, thank you, Sister Padron" is always the answer.

Her response is, "A good Mormon doesn't lie. Now, tell me how you really are!" And the floodgates will open. Tarisse has watched her spend hours in service. For the first visit, Sister Padron might take over a card. She might take a flower on the next. Sometimes she takes a dish of homemade rice-milk pudding that the Latins relish. She listens for hours. She ministers.

Two young women in her Hispanic ward in Southgate are the two last examples I will share. They are both converts to the Church, the only members in their families. They were two of the only members of the ward who had cars. Erika and Veronica came to every meeting they possibly could, their cars full of youth, of families, of the elderly. They spent hours driving ward members all over the place. Did they have nothing else to do with their time? Who wants to spend all their free time taking the missionaries to the grocery store or taking families wherever they need to go? Wouldn't most young people rather spend their free time on the telephone, watching videos, experimenting with hairstyles and makeup with their girlfriends? Playing ball with the guys, skiing, sleeping? Does that sound selfish? It sounds normal to the youth my daughter grew up with. But it is not normal in the culture where she has learned what it means to be a ministering angel.

During the months just before her own mission, Erika not only drove members everywhere, but she was coaxed one evening into lending her car to a group of teens in the ward. None of their families owned cars, and these youth enjoyed the freedom that transportation gives. As they were coming home from a delightful evening, the group headed right into a police barricade where the officers were performing a drug check, and all approaching cars were being pulled over. The teenage driver of Erika's car did not have a license—a major omission under the circumstances.

The teenager panicked and bolted with the carload of friends. The police chased him, and he crashed Erika's car. She had planned to use it until her MTC entrance date and then sell it to pay for part of her mission. If you were Erika and your family had disowned you because of the gospel, and you were doing everything you could to be active, to be supportive of all the members in your ward, wouldn't you have been frustrated? Perhaps you would even have had strong words for the Lord.

Ministering angels do not try to dictate to the Lord how to run his kingdom. They, like the particles of the earth, simply obey. This sweet young woman felt awful for the teenage boy. She knew he felt awful about her car. On top of that, he was cited for not having a license. She took him into her arms, hugged him, and told him it would be okay. And it was. She did sell the car and is now serving as a sister missionary in Texas. Her friend Veronica is serving in Japan.

These two young women did not sell the Lord for silver and gold, for things that thieves could break through and steal. They were ministering angels, and they were focused on being even as Christ is.

Let us join them. Let us allow the Spirit to whisper to us. Let us not be less than the dust of the earth which moves hither and thither to the dividing asunder at the command of our great and everlasting God. "Yea, behold at his voice do the hills and the mountains tremble and quake. And by the power of his voice they are broken up, and become smooth, yea, even like unto a valley. Yea, by the power of his voice doth the whole earth shake; yea, by the power of his voice do the foundations rock, even to the very center" (Helaman 12:8-12). Let us listen and obey and reach out to each other, one by one.

Kathryn Schlendorf *joined the Church when she was fifteen years old. She studied for a year in France and traveled the world with a Brigham Young University group in 1966. She has taught at EFY and in other programs since 1983, and was an early morning seminary teacher for eight years. She teaches English and French at a middle school in Provo, Utah. The mother of four children, Kathryn currently teaches gospel doctrine in her Orem ward.*

5

The Power of Truth: How to Resist, Regroup, and Respond to Temptation

Michael Weir Allred

The letter from Elizabeth read:

Dear Jim,

Last night, you pleaded with me to prove my love for you. You said that when two people really love each other as much as we do, it's only natural to share that love completely. You were very persuasive. And because of the deep feelings I have for you, it was hard to deny you. For hours after I left, I was afraid of losing you—afraid that I had made a terrible mistake. But today, I'm thankful from the depths of my heart that I did not give in to you. I am so relieved that I don't have to bear the terrible burden of having lost my virtue. In the middle of the night, I got up and opened the Book of Mormon to a verse that I had somehow remembered. It's where Mormon is writing to his son, Moroni. I could really feel his horror and sorrow as he told of the terrible cruelty of the Nephite soldiers to the Lamanite maidens. Many of the daughters of the Lamanites had been taken prisoner, he said, and deprived of "that which is most dear and precious above all things, which is chastity and virtue." These words came powerfully into my mind last night. I read them over and over again.

I wonder if I could help you understand, just a little, what you were asking. You are so proud of your new car. What would you say if someone asked you to give up your car as proof of your affection for her? You would think she was joking. If she persisted, you might question her motive or her sincerity. Yet you could get another car. But how could either of us ever know if we would be willing to pay the price, the terrible cost of restoring virtue—yours as well as mine? Last night, you asked me to surrender my purity and self-respect for a few minutes of excitement and pleasure for yourself. Your talk of my proving my love for you was a bitter mockery. If you really love me, you'll have to prove to me that virtue means more to you than pleasure. That you think more of us than you do of yourself.

Elizabeth

(From *Hold to the Rod*, Scripture Motivation and Comprehension Series, Video Presentation 1, "Hold to the Rod," Church Educational System, 1984.)

This letter reflects a common problem. How many times has Satan influenced someone to use the phrase, "If you love me . . ."? In fact, it is so common, why would anyone fall for it? How come so many are deceived into believing that this is love? But what about Elizabeth? She was able to resist, regroup, and respond to the pressures of her boyfriend. Where did her strength come from?

As we analyze the letter's narrative, we see that she was strong enough to resist. That resistance bought her some time. During the time she was alone, thinking about what had just happened, Satan did not stop tempting her. Had she just lost her boyfriend? Would he still love her? Did he really love her in the first place? Had she made the right decision? These kinds of questions were on her mind, making it a sleepless night.

Finally, because of her righteousness, the Spirit prompted her and a scripture came into her mind. She opened her Book of Mormon to the inspired scripture and was strengthened by an understanding of a true doctrine. She gained power through knowing that chastity and virtue are most dear and precious above all things. And, having received this answer from the Lord, there was no way the gates of hell were going to prevail against her. She was able to regroup with the Spirit, getting back to where she needed to be.

Jim had been deceived. Elizabeth discovered the lies and was able to find the truth. She now knew the truth about the value of chastity. She knew the truth about Jim, too—that he was thinking of himself. No wonder the scriptures teach us to gird our loins with truth (Ephesians 6:14). If we only knew the truth, we would see that where there is temptation, there is a lie. Think about it. With truth the phrase would be, "If you love me, if you truly love me, you will want what is best for me: chastity, virtue, and eternal life." The power is in the truth. Elizabeth was able to respond to Jim in a way that might help him to resist the temptations he was feeling and regroup with the Spirit, which he needed so desperately.

Here are three recommendations for receiving eternal truth. They are preparation, pursuit, and power.

PREPARATION: The process of making ready for use.

The first step in obtaining truth is to *prepare* for the truth. Before you can eat a nut, you have to crack the hard shell on the outside. If we are not spiritually prepared, we will not understand spiritual truths, for the natural man thinks that spiritual things are foolishness (see 1 Corinthians 2:14). What good would it do if Heavenly Father gave us spiritual insight when we are not ready to receive it? It would be like a dad giving his two-year-old the keys to the family car.

Here are four elements of preparation required before receiving truth from the Spirit: Desire, Faith, Repentance, and Obedience.

Desire: "But behold, if ye will awake and arouse your faculties, even to an experiment upon my words, and exercise a particle of faith, yea even if ye can no more than *desire* to believe, let this *desire* work in you, even until ye believe in a manner that ye can give place for a portion of my words" (Alma 32:27; emphasis added).

Faith: "And in that day that they shall exercise faith in me, saith the Lord, even as the brother of Jared did . . . then will I manifest unto them the things which the brother of Jared saw, even to the unfolding unto them all my revelations" (Ether 4:7).

Repentance: "And now behold, my brethren, what natural man is there that knoweth these things? I say unto you, there is none that knoweth these things, save it be the penitent" (Alma 26:21).

Obedience: "If any man will do his will, he shall know of the doctrine, whether it be of God, or whether I speak of myself" (John 7:17).

As we prepare ourselves for the truth, we become attuned to spiritual things. We are now ready to learn from the Spirit.

PURSUIT: To adopt measures to obtain.

Once we have prepared ourselves appropriately, we need to seek the truth. We need not suppose that the Lord will just give it to us; we need to do our part (see D&C 9:7-8).

Consider the Missionary Training Center. Why doesn't the Lord just give us the foreign language ability and ship us to our mission field? Why do we have to memorize scriptures? Why doesn't he just put the quotes into our brains? While on my mission, I remember hearing a quote that said, "Together you and the Lord can move mountains, but don't be surprised if he hands you a shovel." Sometimes receiving truth from the Spirit might seem like moving a mountain to get a treasure, but it is a mountain he wants us to move. He wants us to have that treasure.

Here are five suggestions for obtaining truth: Study, Ponder, Pray, Fast, and Apply.

Study: "Search the scriptures; for in them ye think ye have eternal life: and they are they which testify of me" (John 5:39).

President Ezra Taft Benson stressed the importance of studying the gospel when he said, "We should make daily study of the scriptures a lifetime pursuit. . . . The most important [thing] you can do . . . is to immerse yourselves in the scriptures. Search them diligently . . . Learn the doctrine" (*Ensign*, November 1986, p. 47).

Ponder: "This book of the law shall not depart out of thy mouth; but thou shalt meditate therein day and night, that thou mayest observe to do according to all that is written therein: for then thou shalt make thy way prosperous, and then thou shalt have good success" (Joshua 1:8).

We need to understand that "the things of God are of vast importance, and require time and experience as well as deep and solemn thought to find them out" (Joseph Smith, Hyrum Smith, Lyman Wight, *Times and Seasons*, May 1840, p. 102; cited in Rulon T. Burton, *We Believe: Doctrines and Principles of The Church of Jesus Christ of Latter-day Saints* [Salt Lake City: Tabernacle Books, 1994], p. 1071).

Pray: "If any of you lack wisdom, let him ask of God, that giveth to all men liberally, and upbraideth not; and it shall be given him" (James 1:5).

Joseph Smith said, "The best way to obtain truth and wisdom is not to ask it from books, but to go to God in prayer and obtain divine teaching" (*Teachings of the Prophet Joseph Smith* [Salt Lake City: Deseret Book Co., 1938], p. 191).

Fast: "Behold, I say unto you they are made known unto me by the Holy Spirit of God. Behold, I have fasted and prayed many days that I might know these things of myself. And now I do know of myself that they are true; for the Lord God hath made them manifest unto me by his Holy Spirit; and this is the spirit of revelation which is in me" (Alma 5:46).

Apply: "Therefore whosoever heareth these sayings of mine, *and doeth them*, I will liken him unto a wise man, which built his house upon a rock" (Matthew 7:24; emphasis added).

As we seek the truth by studying, pondering, fasting, praying, and applying the truth in our lives, we open a treasure that lasts forever. The more we find, the more there is, until we have all that our Father in Heaven has. That is the way he wants it.

POWER: Strength to act, produce, and perform.

The reception of truth shows up in many ways. (See Matthew 7:16.) One of the fruits of truth is power. Have you ever considered that there are many things we plug into electrical power? The power is the same, but the application depends on what is plugged in. So it is with truth. The Spirit blesses us with truth, which gives us the strength to act, produce, and perform. Notice that this power shows up in various areas of our lives:

Power to Resist:

—The desire for sin.

"The nearer man approaches perfection, the clearer are his views, and the greater his enjoyments, till he has overcome the evils of his life and lost every desire for sin." *(Teachings of the Prophet Joseph Smith,* p. 51)

—The gates of hell.

"Then said Jesus to those Jews which believed on him, If ye continue in my word, then are ye my disciples indeed; And ye shall know the truth, and the truth shall make you free." (John 8:31-32)

President Harold B. Lee taught that "truth is the scepter of power, which if man possesses, will give him 'dominion' and the ability to 'subdue all things'" (*We Believe*, p. 1076). This power is so vital that we should not fail to obtain it. President Joseph F. Smith said, "The greatest achievement mankind can make in this world is to familiarize themselves with divine truth, so thoroughly, so perfectly, that the example or conduct of no creature living in the world can ever turn them away from the knowledge that they have obtained" (Joseph F. Smith, *Gospel Doctrine* [Salt Lake City: Deseret Book Co., 1939], pp. 3-4). And listen to the words of Helaman to his sons:

And now, my sons, remember, remember that it is upon the rock of our Redeemer, who is Christ, the Son of God, that ye must build your foundation; that when the devil shall send forth his mighty winds, yea, his shafts in the whirlwind, yea, when all his hail and his mighty storm shall beat upon you, it shall have no power over you to drag you down to the gulf of misery and endless wo, because of the rock upon which ye are built, which is a sure foundation, a foundation whereon if men build they cannot fall. (Helaman 5:12)

Power to Regroup:

—To receive more truth.

"And therefore, he that will harden his heart, the same receiveth the lesser portion of the word; and he that will not harden his heart, to him is given the greater portion of the word, until it is given unto him to know the mysteries of God until he know them in full." (Alma 12:10)

—To become the children of God.

"But verily, verily, I say unto you, that as many as receive me, to them will I give power to become the Sons [and daughters] of God, even to them that believe on my name. Amen." (D&C 11:30)

Elder Bruce R. McConkie said, "We have the power—and it is our privilege—so to live, that becoming pure in heart, we shall see the face of God while we yet dwell as mortals in a world of sin and sorrow" (*Conference Report*, October 1977, p. 34).

Power to Respond:

—To teach with the Spirit.

"But this is not all; they had given themselves to much prayer, and fasting; therefore they had the spirit of prophecy, and the spirit of revelation, and when they taught, they taught with power and authority of God."(Alma 17:3)

—To teach with power.

"And now, as the preaching of the word had a great tendency to lead the people to do that which was just—yea, it had had more powerful effect upon the minds of the people than the sword, or anything else, which had happened unto them—therefore Alma thought it was expedient that they should try the virtue of the word of God." (Alma 31:5)

As we participate in this power, we realize its effect on us and those we serve. This real knowledge of the past, present, and future blesses us with a confidence that is manifest in many areas of our lives (see D&C 93:24). We are able to resist temptation, regroup with the Spirit, and respond to those who need our help.

In 2 Timothy 3:16, we learn that all scripture is given by inspiration and is profitable for man in the areas of doctrine, reproof, correction, and instruction. Knowing the doctrine, we understand truth. We are reproved when out of harmony with the truth, and then we are corrected as needed and instructed in paths of righteousness.

Our Eternal Father wants us to learn and know his doctrine. He "and His Beloved Son are willing, even anxious for us to learn from them. . . . Gaining spiritual knowledge is not a mechanical process. It is a sacred privilege based upon spiritual law" (Richard G. Scott, *Ensign*, November 1993, p. 88).

We need to be in constant pursuit of truth in order to possess its power. The Lord wants us to obtain his truths so that we may stand up to temptation. We, like Elizabeth, should not wait to prepare. Elizabeth had already learned her response to temptation, and the Spirit drew it out in her time of need. The scriptures teach us to treasure up the truths that will give us spiritual power: "Neither take ye thought beforehand what ye shall say; but treasure up in your minds continually the words of life, and it shall be given you in the very hour that portion that shall be meted unto every man" (D&C 84:85).

In conclusion, I would like to share a thought about the importance of knowing the truth.

He who knows not that he knows not—is a fool;
Shun him.
He who knows that he knows not—is seeking;
Teach him.
He who knows not that he knows—is asleep;
Awake him.
He who knows that he knows—is a wise man;
Follow him.

Arabian Proverb

May we treasure the truth by our personal preparation to receive truth, by our energetic pursuit of truth, and by our use of the power of truth.

Michael Weir Allred *teaches seminary at Roy High School in Ogden, Utah, and one class in Japanese at the Ogden Institute. He is a graduate of Weber State University and the University of Phoenix. Before becoming a teacher, he served in the Army National Guard as a counterintelligence agent and Japanese interpreter. Brother Allred enjoys playing the drums and has taught drum lessons. He claims to love all sports, "even synchronized swimming." He and his wife, Kathy, have four children, and he says he is currently developing skills to become a better home teacher.*

6

Asleep at the Gate

David L. Buckner

The sign-up sheet had gone around the class three times, and still no one had volunteered for the Saturday food distribution in Harlem. Once again the list landed in my hands, and I felt that uncomfortable feeling you get when you know you could help but you just don't feel like taking the time. I passed it on one more time and within a few minutes, it landed again in my hands. I felt a knot in my stomach as I remembered that oft-quoted scripture from Matthew 25:40: "Inasmuch as ye have done it unto one of the least of these my brethren, ye have done it unto me."

Okay, okay, I said to myself. *I'll do it.* Then glancing heavenward, I muttered, "Are you happy now?"

The next Saturday morning at 11:30 a.m. I arrived at the stake center in the heart of New York City just in time to begin unloading the food boxes from the transport truck into the delivery cars. I was assigned to Brother Austin, who would be my driver, and we began our trek into the Harlem neighborhoods of New York City. Although I had agreed to participate in the service project, I was less than enthusiastic about the prospects of driving through such a rough part of town and dropping off food to those considered to be "needy." After all, this was Saturday, "my day"—not a day I wanted to waste on service projects or church outings.

Our first stop was in a really rough neighborhood. A shrine of flowers had been placed on one corner and was dedicated to a young boy who had been shot and killed there earlier in the week. I was uncomfortable with the whole feeling of the street, so I grabbed the boxes of food for delivery and hurried through the open gate into the narrow halls of the unlighted housing tenement. The halls were dark and there were a number of young kids just "hanging out," speaking an English slang I had never heard before.

When I found the apartment we were looking for, I knocked on the door and was greeted with the sounds of a ferocious dog barking.

"Who is it?" a woman's voice called.

"I'm from the Church," I said. "I have your food." The door opened a crack and then closed slightly as she undid the four locks and allowed me to enter. I put the food on the small table in the center of the room and thanked her for allowing me in her home. I left with little else being said.

After I climbed back into the car, Brother Austin quickly sped on to the next drop-off point. One by one we made our deliveries, encountering a unique set of circumstances at each stop. At our final stop, we pulled up in front of what appeared to be a bombed-out building; it was merely a hollow shelter with a few windows and missing doors. The front door of the building, one of the few that remained, was without lock or handle, and covered with graffiti. I pushed open the door and entered a long, dark hallway. It was clear no one had made any effort to clean or repair the building or make it safe. The halls were painted pea-soup green and covered with graffiti markings. The staircase was missing its hand railing, which was lying on the floor below, and the locks on the apartment doors resembled bank vaults rather than homes or residences. The smell of decaying walls, leaking chemicals, and septic tanks permeated the air as I hiked the three floors to the apartment of Dotsie, a tall black woman with a smile as wide and beautiful as a sunset. She opened the door and welcomed me into her home. The hallway smells were now replaced with smells of home cooking, but the general decor and lighting were no different than those I had seen all day.

There was, however, one small but very significant difference. Just as I placed the goods on the table, I turned to leave and saw out of the corner of my eye a picture of our Savior over the mantle, the same picture I have seen in chapels across the country. And yet, in this setting, it was different. It wasn't just a picture to enhance the decor. It was a declaration of faith, a testimony amid the violence, a message to all who entered Dotsie's home that her Elder Brother was welcome there. No gold, no silver, no riches, just an incredible love for her Savior, Jesus Christ, and a continuing hope and firm belief that someday soon he will again return.

I felt a bit emotional as I looked around me and began to feel the power of the Spirit fill this humble home. The simple prompting I had received the previous Sunday was much clearer now: "Inasmuch as ye have done it unto the least of these my brethren, ye have done it unto me." Was it the Savior I was serving that day? Or had he actually been serving me?

COMING UNTO CHRIST

Time and time again we have been taught that we must "come unto Christ." We must learn of him, become like him, and strive to return to him. All too often we assume this means simply attending our church meetings weekly or paying our tithing. We form a checklist in our minds that guides us through all the Primary and Sunday School answers we were taught. Come unto Christ? Sure, all you have to do is pray, read your scriptures, go to church and "be good." But what happens when we are called in the middle of the night by a friend in need of help or advice? What happens when we are asked to spend time caring for young children or elderly loved ones without pay or reward? And what happens when we are asked to participate in a quorum service project that will take the better part of our Saturday? What happens if it isn't convenient or doesn't fit into our checklist?

Our Church leaders have reminded us repeatedly that it is through sacrifice and service that we will come to know the Lord. When we put aside our own desires and serve God and others, we become more like our Father in Heaven. As we learn to rise above our wish for comfort and satisfaction, we become closer to God and his Son Jesus Christ.

My visit to Dotsie's home began to change my heart as well as my thinking. It was clear to me that Dotsie understood much more than many of us who have been members of the Church all our lives. She had a true desire to "come unto Christ," to learn of him, become like him, and strive endlessly to return to him. Her humble home was filled with happiness, joy, and the Spirit of the Lord. Although she had been a member of the Church for less than a year, she had come to understand her latter-day calling, a calling described in the final few verses of Moroni: "Yea come unto Christ, and be perfected in him, and deny yourselves of all ungodliness" (Moroni 10:32).

Struggle, sacrifice, service—of course I was familiar with such gospel concepts. But standing in that humble home, peering up at our Savior's face and reflecting on his struggle, sacrifice, and service, I felt I had never really understood how important these principles are, especially in these latter-days.

Every day of our lives we must face a world filled with challenges to meet, battles to fight, and struggles to overcome. After all, this is that time in history often written of by the prophets of old. You are that very select group of young warriors chosen to come down in this dispensation, at this time, and to your particular homes. Your calling is clear. You are to usher in the Second Coming of Jesus Christ. Your mission call has been issued to you by our Father in Heaven through his prophet Joseph Smith as he declared "Prepare ye, prepare ye, O inhabitants of the earth; for the judgment of our God is come" (D&C 88:92). You have been instructed that as you stand as a witness to the many events of the latter days, and you have, you "shall know that he is near, even at the doors" (Joseph Smith Translation—Matthew 1:39). That is why we have been commanded to "come unto Christ." Not simply to read about or discuss him on Sundays, but actually bring ourselves unto him, know him, become like him.

But how is this done? How can we physically and spiritually get closer to our Elder Brother, Jesus Christ? How do we become perfected in him and deny ourselves of all ungodliness?

Too often we see such a task as an impossible goal or objective. After all, we say to ourselves, "nobody's perfect." But there is a way.

In fact, we have been promised that we can become perfected in him, our sins can be forgiven us, and we can be truly purified if we learn to come unto Christ through sacrifice and service. For "sanctification . . . is just and true, to all those who love and serve God with all their mights, minds and strength" (D&C 20:31). *Sacrifice* and *service*—are those just words we use when we're trying to get people to volunteer for something they really don't want to do? It's just another Saturday morning food project all over again—or is it?

SELFLESS SACRIFICE

Not long ago, Elder Ballard, a member of the Quorum of the Twelve Apostles, was assigned to preside over and speak at a Church regional conference in La Paz, Bolivia. Members traveled from far-off towns and small villages to attend the conference. A number of members had to sacrifice much time, effort, and money to get to the meetings so they could listen to the words of an apostle of God.

Prior to the Saturday evening meeting, Elder Ballard stood in front of the chapel to greet many of the arriving brethren. He noticed several brethren arriving somewhat disheveled and tired after what must have been a very long journey. As they approached the beloved apostle, he noticed the discoloration of the brothers' shirts. From mid-chest above, the shirts maintained a clean white appearance. However, from mid-chest and below, the white fabric had become discolored and stained with a reddish coloring. When they approached to shake his hand, they informed him that they were so pleased to have arrived in time to meet him. They had spent many hours traveling to the meetings, much of that time on foot. They were required to ford two rivers along the way where the reddish water came up to their chests. The final two hours had been spent riding in the back of a pickup truck. As they greeted Elder Ballard, they humbly offered a lesson in sacrifice. "Elder Ballard," they said, "you are one of the Lord's Apostles. My brethren and I would do whatever was required to be taught by you" ("The Law of Sacrifice" address given at the 1996 New Testament Symposium, 13 August 1996, Brigham Young University, Provo, Utah).

Why do we find it so difficult to attend our Sunday meetings, get up for early-morning seminary, or participate in Church-sponsored activities or service opportunities? Why is it so hard to give up a moment of popularity in order to keep our bodies free from abusive substances, or our virtue intact? Why are we so compelled by money, our possessions, and other worldly things? And why do we find it so easy to say, "It's just too hard to do?"

It is all a part of the adversary's plan for our downfall. More than anything else in this world, Satan is set on taking away our gift of choice and thus destroy our eternal progression.

The Lord's plan allows us to succeed on our own, to prove our worthiness to return to him, and to demonstrate our ability to sacrifice the immediate for the eternal. This is the only way we are able to preserve our gift of choice. We must learn to sacrifice the immediate for the eternal. All too often we stand idly by, hoping that others will sign up for the service project, or that our presence will not be missed at church meetings or seminary classes. We forget that by doing this, we are giving away our gift of choice. We are suggesting that we are unwilling to demonstrate our faith by choosing to sacrifice or postpone gratification. But we must learn to rise above our love for comfort and ease, and actively commit ourselves to sacrifice our selfish desires. In all that we say, in all that we do, let us learn at a young age to "come unto Christ" by learning how to sacrifice.

CEASELESS SERVICE

The sun was setting and the sounds of the public festival could be heard in the distance. Having just completed their evening meal, the twelve men began their stroll under the star-filled skies. They passed through the city gate, which was always left open during the festival week, and proceeded toward the small ravine that separated the city from the orchards on the adjoining hill. Although the festival sounds rang out in the darkness of the night, there was a heaviness that had beset those in the group. They had been warned of what would transpire that evening, and their hearts were heavy and their moods somber as they anticipated the events to follow.

This was no ordinary after-dinner stroll. Their company had been specially requested by the leader of their group. Unlike other nights, he had asked them to accompany him out of the city to a quiet place where he had often gone alone before. They crossed the small ravine and entered an orchard of trees. The gnarled trunks branched out into large sprawling limbs adorned with a savory fruit that supplied precious oil to all in the area.

The leader of the group asked eight of his friends to wait at the gate and keep watch for him. He warned them that they might be tempted to leave their watch, but again asked, more fervently now, that they resist such impulses and stay attentive while he continued further into the orchard. He took with him the three remaining colleagues and entered the garden of trees to search for a place of peace and quiet. As they proceeded, he felt the need to be alone and asked that his three remaining friends wait for him as he continued on.

Before going, he stopped and again asked that they wait and watch with him. He warned them that they might also be tempted to rest their eyes or leave their post. He pleaded with them to stay alert and watch while he sat off in the distance. The more ambitious of the three promised to do as he had been asked. Earlier in the night, this very same friend had boastfully promised to do anything asked of him; he had assured the group that nothing could make him waiver in his commitment to his leader.

Having denied himself the companionship of his closest friends, his disciples, the Master went into the garden, fell on his face, and prayed to the Father: "O my Father, if it be possible, let this cup pass from me: nevertheless not as I will, but as thou wilt" (Matthew 26:34). His greatest service to all humankind was now taking place. The greatest event of all time was now occurring. Yet, when the Master returned to the gate, he found that those whom he had trusted to serve him in his hour of need had forgotten his instructions and ceased to serve. In the hour of his deepest humiliation, his closest friends were found asleep at the gate. The Master called to Peter, who only a short time before had loudly and boastfully proclaimed his willingness to follow his Master even to prison and death. Awakening Peter, Christ asked, "What, could ye not watch with me one hour?" (Matthew 26:40). Compassionately he then added, "The spirit is indeed willing, but the flesh is weak."

After awakening all his disciples, the Master again asked that they stay awake and watch with him, then retired to continue praying to the Father. After a short period he again returned, only to find all the apostles again asleep at the gate. This time they awakened, embarrassed and ashamed, for they knew he had begged them to watch and wait with him.

A third time he left his friends to return to his lonely vigil. And yet a third time their eyes were heavy, and for a third time the Lord returned to find them asleep at the gate. This time instead of awakening them, he simply said, "Sleep on now, and take your rest: behold, the hour is at hand, and the Son of man is betrayed into the hands of sinners" (Matthew 26:45) and they continued to sleep at the gate. (See James Talmage, *Jesus the Christ* [Salt Lake City: Deseret Book, 1986], p. 610-12.)

That night in Gethsemane, the Savior of the world atoned for the sins of all mankind. The greatest event in the history of this world occurred while those who professed to love him most slept quietly at the gate.

How often do we, who profess to love our Elder Brother, who take upon ourselves his name at baptism and recommit weekly to always remember him, how often are we found quietly sleeping at the gate? How often have we thought of Peter's actions at the gate and said to ourselves, "I would never have betrayed His confidence or disobeyed His wishes. I would never have slept while the Master bled from every pore." Yet we may frequently dismiss the needs of our family, our friends, our neighbors, and other human beings. As the volunteer list is passed our way, we may think of reasons why we can't serve, why our time is too precious with none to spare, why our needs are greater than the needs of others. We may avoid the late-night telephone calls from those in need of advice or fellowship. We may dismiss acts of charity or kindness as burdensome and inconvenient. We may disregard those who are looking for friendship, support, and a sense of belonging, choosing instead to exclude or distance ourselves from the burden of making new friends. At times we become consumed by our school work, our jobs, or our social activities and forget our purpose in life. In all these ways we slowly but surely find ourselves fast asleep at the gate.

A month had now passed since my first visit to Dotsie's home. As the sign-up sheet came my way, I saw that a number of spaces were now filled in. Those brethren who had participated in the Harlem food distribution had returned to recount the wonderful experiences they had had, which had prompted many to sign the list. When the list landed in my hands, I took out the pencil and quickly filled in all the remaining spaces with my name. While this act may have seemed noble, I knew better. This service was not a burden; it was a blessing. For too many years, I had found myself asleep at the gate, watching as others built the kingdom around me. Now it was my turn to sacrifice. It was my turn to keep watch, to "come unto Christ." This time the Master would not have to say, "Sleep on now, and take your rest: behold, the hour is at hand, and the Son of man is betrayed into the hands of sinners." No, I would not be found sleeping at the gate.

In these latter days we have been asked to stand at the gate and prepare for the second coming of our Elder Brother Jesus Christ. There is no time to waste, there is no chance to sleep. We must commit ourselves today to live righteously, to share our knowledge of the gospel freely and openly, to search the scriptures fervently, to pray endlessly and to love and serve unconditionally. As we catch this vision, it is my prayer that we may learn to sacrifice and serve our fellow beings without ceasing. For "inasmuch as ye have done it unto one of the least of these my brethren, ye have done it unto me."

In all that we say, in all that we do, let us learn at a young age to "come unto Christ," by learning how to actively serve every day of our lives with all our heart, might, mind, and strength. It is my continued prayer that as we prepare for His arrival, we may become consumed with the desire to sacrifice and serve our brothers and sisters and, in turn, our Savior. I bear witness of these marvelous principles of light and life. Your life will truly change and your testimony will grow and develop as you come unto Christ.

David L. Buckner *graduated from Brigham Young University with a degree in international finance and a masters in international relations. After obtaining an MBA from Durham University in England, he attended and graduated from Brigham Young University Law School. David currently serves as gospel doctrine teacher in his Manhattan Ward as well as Stake Director of Seminaries. He and his wife, Jennifer, have two wonderful sons, Joshua and Matthew. David enjoys snow skiing, traveling, scuba diving, tennis, current events, history, politics, film, art, and Broadway theater. Most of all, he enjoys speaking to the youth of the Church..*

7

THE LORD'S "LOST AND FOUND"

Kim N. Gunnell

"Get that gross stuff off me," Casey complained as I attempted to apply lotion to his dry, chapped hands. Casey, our youngest son, was about seven years old when he developed a rash-like condition on his hands that wouldn't go away. The doctor assured me that Casey would heal just by using lotion regularly, but Casey didn't want anything to do with that "gross stuff."

At times his poor hands would chap to the point of bleeding and I would plead with him to let me put lotion on them. He would just jerk away, wipe his hands on his jeans, and say, "Yuck! I don't want that sissy stuff on my hands." One evening while the family was snuggling on the sofa watching a video, I reached for some lotion and inconspicuously tried to rub some on Casey's hands while he was watching the movie. The minute Casey smelled the lotion he shouted, "Mom, don't even think about it!"

Later that night I discussed my concerns with my husband, Doug. He suggested that since he read to Casey and his brother every night, he could simply wait till the boys were asleep and then gently rub some Vaseline™—the heavy-duty stuff—on Casey's hands. The following night Doug began his secret mission. After Casey had fallen asleep, Doug reached under the covers and ever so carefully pulled out one of Casey's hands. Carefully, so as to not wake him, he rubbed in the Vaseline™. Then he slipped that hand under the covers and pulled out the other hand. Doug continued the compassionate ritual for several nights and the plan worked. We saw a dramatic difference in Casey's hands—even Casey noticed. He said, "Hey, my hands don't even hurt anymore." When we finally confessed to Casey, he just said, "I guess that's okay as long as I'm asleep."

The following Sunday was fast and testimony meeting, and Doug shared his testimony. Then he briefly told the story of Casey's hands. I wondered why on earth he was telling that story until he concluded by saying, "Being a man, I don't really take good care of my hands either. When I work in the garden my hands become pretty chapped, and I don't like the smell of lotion any more than Casey. My hands were in pretty bad shape when I began caring for my son's hands. But as I helped my son's hands to heal, I noticed that my hands were healing too."

Doug learned that you can't put lotion on another's hands without also getting some on your own. You can't help another without also helping yourself. The Savior said, "He that findeth his life shall lose it: and he that loseth his life for my sake shall find it" (Matthew 10:39). Apparently, that principle is so important it is repeated several times in the scriptures (see Matthew 16:25; Mark 8:35; Luke 9:24; 17:33). It is only when we lose ourselves in serving others that we truly find ourselves.

When you lose something you value—a wallet or purse, a camera, or your scriptures—what is the first thing you do to try to find them? You check the lost and found. If I lose something, I hope someone will be kind enough to return what I have lost so I can find it again, but there is always a chance that whatever I have lost will be lost forever. But the Lord's "lost and found" is different. As I lose my life in selfless attention and service to others, I *will* find a better life and that's a 100 percent, full-proof, no-fail guarantee!

One young man named Clark also learned the truth of this principle when he was invited by a young woman to attend the girls' choice dance at his college. She was tall, athletic, and probably threatened most young men her age. She didn't date very much, and her roommates had talked her into taking a date to the dance. It took all her courage, but she finally invited Clark to go with her. When Clark's buddies found out about the invitation, they teased him mercilessly. "You're not *really* going with her, are you?" asked one.

Another said, "I wouldn't be caught dead in public with that giant."

Inside, Clark worried about what people might think or say if he went out with this girl. He worried about his own image and popularity at college, but he worried more about this young woman's feelings and self-esteem. Despite his own fears and the jokes of his buddies, Clark attended the dance and had a wonderful evening. He and the young lady discovered they had much in common and became friends.

During later college years the young woman began receiving a lot of attention from the national news media as she received several prestigious awards in athletics. Suddenly, Clark's buddies weren't cracking jokes anymore. In fact, Clark's friends were envious when Clark received complimentary tickets to attend the Olympics where his friend would be competing.

Clark initially felt like he was making a small sacrifice to go out with this girl. However, Clark soon discovered that his popularity and status were not hurt in the least. He didn't lose anything. On the contrary, he found a friendship that enriched his life for years.

I have a friend named Brad, who as an eight-year-old faced a difficult adjustment when his family moved back to the United States after living overseas. Brad did not grow up playing ball since sports weren't emphasized where he had been living. Suddenly, in his American school, Brad found himself feeling left out at recess. He was always chosen last when team members were picked for basketball or baseball. In fact, the team members would usually fight over which team was going to get stuck with Brad. Pretty soon Brad simply stopped playing altogether and turned his attention to music and other interests.

When Brad entered seventh grade he faced another difficult transition. The students in junior high came from several different elementary schools, and many who suffered from insecurity picked on others. Somehow, in the shuffle, Brad ended up at the bottom of the pecking order. Each day he had to face the threats, rejection, and hurtful criticisms of classmates.

In addition, the PE class most boys looked forward to was the one he dreaded the most. One day the regular coach wasn't there and the class was covered by a substitute who divided the group into relay teams. He explained that each team member would be expected to run to the other side of the gym, climb the rope, and run back. The first team finished would win. Eagerly, the boys lined up and Brad made his way to the back of his line. He knew he couldn't climb the rope. The top of the rope might as well have been the top of the World Trade Center.

"Ready, set, go!" The coach blew his whistle and the race began. In the heat of competition, the boys yelled wildly for their teammates. Helplessly, Brad awaited his turn—his heart thumping in fear. As he got closer to the front of the line, Brad worked out a plan in his mind: He would run as fast as he could, grab the rope, and pull himself up until the coach wasn't looking. Then he could slide down and run back to his place. He didn't want his teammates losing the race because of him.

When his turn in the relay came, he ran to the rope and pulled with all his strength. He could hardly lift himself above the ground. His arms shook as he struggled just to hold on. Brad glanced toward the coach who wasn't watching and let go of the rope. He dropped to the ground and was running back to his place when suddenly, to his horror, the coach blew his whistle and started yelling. Everyone stopped and the gym grew silent.

The coach pointed at Brad and yelled, "All right, young man. We will have no cheating in this race! Get back to that rope and climb it all the way to the top." In humiliation, Brad returned to the rope as the entire class gathered to watch. Amid the smirks and laughter of his peers, Brad began struggling unsuccessfully to climb the rope until at last he was rescued by the shower bell.

Because of this horrible experience, Brad could have become angry. He could have quit school. He could have taken his frustration out on the coach or other students. He could have become depressed and withdrawn. Instead, Brad made a vow to himself that he would never treat anyone else like that. He determined to always try to treat others with respect and kindness.

In the years that followed, Brad noticed when others were suffering. There was a boy with a birth defect that left his face somewhat deformed who was shy and awkward. Brad went out of his way to find the boy in the hall and sit by him in classes. The young man worked in the lunchroom scraping trays. Brad signed up to work there, too, so the boy wouldn't be alone.

On another occasion Brad overheard a group of girls gossiping about another girl named Jenny. One girl asked, "Did you hear the news about Jenny? She's moving!"

Another girl flipped her hair and said, "I'm glad because I can't stand her."

Yet another joined in saying, "She bugs me too! She thinks she's so neat and she's not! I'm glad we won't have to put up with her anymore."

Brad decided that Jenny didn't need people talking about her as much as she might need friends. He gathered some of the young people in his ward and put together a surprise going-away party to wish Jenny well in her new school.

Brad began to lose his life in quiet, sincere service to others, and just as the scriptures promise, he began to find his life. The more Brad worried about others, the less he worried about himself and the more he began to be accepted by his peers. In fact, when he got to high school, he was selected by all the girls in the school as one of the most preferred men—the guy they all wanted to go out with.

What had caused such a change? Had he bought a super car? No, he drove an old heap of a Chevy. Had he become a super athlete? No, he still couldn't climb a rope. Had he become a super stud? No, not really—even though he claims he is a dead ringer for Tom Cruise. Brad just became super nice. He knew everyone's name at school. He didn't link himself to this group or that group; he was friendly to all the students. He went out of his way to defend the underdog, compliment others, and find the good in everyone.

Throughout high school he received many awards and honors, but the one that meant the most to him was given at his senior dinner dance. Brad was not named "Most Likely to Succeed" nor was he given the award for being the smartest or coolest. Brad was named the "Most Loved Senior," and as he walked to the front of the room his classmates stood and applauded. Imagine—a standing ovation from some of the very young people who had teased and ridiculed him in junior high.

The first time I met Brad was right after I completed my year as Miss Provo and had begun touring the country with the LDS musical *My Turn on Earth*. In the middle of the tour, one of the male performers left for his mission, and the director of the play began looking for a replacement. When Brad auditioned, I remember thinking, "I hope this guy doesn't get picked. He's not right for the part. He's not athletic enough."

Despite my concerns, Brad was cast in the play, and I wanted the director to know I was not happy about our new male lead. After all, I had to kiss this guy every night during the play! So I was late to the first cast meeting—deliberately.

I rang the doorbell at the director's home, and to my surprise, Brad answered. He flung the door open, leaped toward me, and smothered me in the biggest bear hug I have ever received. He hugged me until my eyelashes were smashed against my face. Before I could say anything, Brad blurted out, "You're gorgeous! I love you, Miss Provo!" I was stunned at how warm and funny he was. Despite my initial impressions of Brad, I found myself really liking him.

I wanted to kick myself for being so unfair in my earlier judgment. I hadn't been very nice to him, and I'm sure he could tell how I was feeling when he auditioned. Still, he didn't give me the chance to be mean. He was so good at loving people that he even loved me when I didn't particularly like him. His sincere kindness melted me, and I couldn't help but begin to love him back. I came to better understand the scripture recorded in 1 John 4:19 where we read of the Savior: "We love him, because he first loved us."

I had to teach Brad how to kiss for the play, but we soon became close friends. After the tour was over Brad left on his mission, and while he was gone I met and married my husband. When Brad returned I was anxious for him to meet Doug and warned my husband that Brad would probably hug him—which he always does and which he did then. We had invited Brad over for dinner, and afterwards Brad said, "Kim, I really love your husband." Then he turned to Doug and said, "Do you happen to have a twin sister I could marry?"

Doug laughed and answered, "As a matter of fact, I do. She'll be home from her mission in a few weeks." Any fairy tale couldn't have had a better ending. Brad met Doug's twin sister, Debi, and they got married. Now Brad and I are twins-in-law!

Had I continued to judge Brad and not accept him I could have lost a great friend. Because I stopped worrying about my own selfish concerns and followed Brad's example of love, look at what I found! I not only found a friend, but also a brother—literally—who will now be part of my eternal family. Our spouses are twins. Our children are cousins. We work together, play together, sing together, spend holidays together. We really love each other. I'm going to be getting those bear hugs through all eternity!

I'm grateful for what I learned about the Lord's "lost and found," for it is only when we lose ourselves that we truly find ourselves. Then, like the father of the prodigal son, the Lord can say of us, "For this my [child] was dead, and is alive again; [my child] was lost, and is found" (Luke 15:24).

A former Mrs. Utah, ***Kim Novas Gunnell*** *was born in Blackfoot, Idaho, and attended Brigham Young University. A homemaker and former Brigham Young Universtiy Young Ambassador, she enjoys scuba diving, water and snow skiing, decorating and crafts, and teaching an institute class with her husband. She sings professionally, and is the choir director in her ward. She currently lives in American Fork, Utah, with her husband, Doug, and three children—Ashley, Barrett, and Casey.*

8

Preparation Is Power

Mark D. Ogletree

When I was in about the third grade, my family and I lived in San Antonio, Texas. For spring break that year, it was decided that we would take our new boat to Padre Island, which is located just off the Texas coast in the Gulf of Mexico. My dad determined that once we launched the boat, we would travel in a southern direction, miles away from civilization. That was his idea of a good time; mine was Disneyland.

Although my dad was about 100 pounds lighter than the "Skipper," and I really didn't resemble "Gilligan" in any way (except for the goofy haircut), I am sure we looked like the crew of the *SS Minnow* as we headed out of Corpus Christi for a three-day "tour." After we had traveled for quite some time and it was evident that we were very far away from anyone, we docked our boat and set up our campsite on the most desolate stretch of beach I had ever seen in my life. There was literally nothing for miles but beach, sand, and seagulls. After the boat was unloaded and our campsite was set up, we went to explore our newfound playground. It didn't take long to notice the interesting sulphur-like smell in the air; we eventually got used to it, but that didn't keep us kids from affectionately naming our little oasis "Stinky Island."

Except for the smell, "Stinky Island" was great. We played on the beach for hours, making sand castles, mud pies, and burying each other with sand and mud. When we weren't doing that, we were playing in the water, swimming under our boat (which we thought was totally cool) and getting stung by jellyfish. It was a kids' paradise, except for the jellyfish, sand, and salt water. Meanwhile, my mom and dad were enjoying the sun, reading good books, having some good uninterrupted conversation, and loving the fact that the closest phone was about fifty miles away. This was a great family vacation. Everything was perfect—until it was time to leave.

We loaded up the boat and prepared for our journey back to society. We were sad to leave, but also anxious to get home. After all, having sand in your pants for three days gets a little old after a while. However, when my dad tried to start the boat, nothing happened. The motor wouldn't even turn over. It became evident that the battery was totally dead!

Now, when you have a dead battery on a boat, there are not many options for getting it running again. Unlike my Ford Escort, push-starting is out of the question. So, my dad did the only thing that he knew was possible: he took the cover of the motor off and tried to start the boat manually (by pulling a rope like on a lawn mower). Nothing happened. He must have tried for hours to start the motor, but it was a total waste of time. Not understanding the severity of the situation, all of us kids jumped out of the boat and began to frolic in the water. The only thing this setback meant to us was that we might get to miss a day of school. Meanwhile, our parents worked frantically on the boat, trying to get it started.

The next day, my dad tried plan "B." He loaded us all in the boat again, tied a rope to the stern, and began to pull the boat out into the Gulf. His hope was that if he could get the boat out far enough, someone would see us. Of course we were a little skeptical, because we hadn't seen another boat in days. To this day, I still remember that scene: I was sitting on the front of the boat, and my dad was walking, struggling, and pulling, trying to get this huge boat out to the shipping lanes. However, once the water was over his head, he really wasn't able to swim and pull the boat, which was loaded with supplies and a family. Finally, exhausted, he climbed into the boat and dried off. Then he told us that all we could do was wait and hope.

I don't remember being that nervous because I was too young, but I am sure my parents felt some great anxiety. Here they were, in the middle of the Gulf of Mexico, with three small children and few, if any, supplies left. Later that day, my dad came out of the cabin of our boat with a pistol. My brother and I almost started crying, because we figured that he was going to shoot us and either A) eat us, or B) chop us up and use us for bait. Luckily, my dad explained that he was going to fire the pistol into the air, in hopes that someone would hear us and come to our aid. Eventually, boats did come into our area, but they were still a mile or two away and probably couldn't see us. My dad would fire his pistol, but no one ever responded. By now, we had missed two days of school.

The situation was becoming hopeless. We were stranded out in the ocean, and it seemed that no one was going to find us. Suddenly, missing more school didn't seem important. I was actually hoping just to see my house and school again.

Thankfully, our hope turned into reality. The next day, my dad spotted a boat that was closer than any boat had been in three days. By this time we were out of bullets, so he resorted to plan "C": waving a dish towel in the air. Finally, and I will never forget it, the boat that we were trying to signal raised its front end out of the water and came speeding towards us. In an instant, help had arrived. Soon our battery was charged, and we cruised back very slowly to Corpus Christi. I will never forget how good it felt to get home, take a shower, and sleep in my own bed.

It wasn't until years later that I began to process what happened to us on "Stinky Island." I realized that we really had not been prepared for a disaster. We could have brought extra food, water, and even a spare battery, but we didn't. From "Stinky Island" and other experiences in my life, I have learned that when we are unprepared, there will always be suffering of some kind. Luckily for my family, our suffering was nothing more than eating Vienna sausages for three days. But what if we'd had to go a few more days until we were discovered? I am glad we didn't have to find out. I am also thankful that in the Church, the Lord has seen fit, through his prophets, to warn us to be prepared—not only temporally with food storage and other supplies, but spiritually as well.

RESERVOIRS: A DEFINITION

I have always been impressed with this statement from President Spencer W. Kimball. Consider his words:

> There are in our lives reservoirs of many kinds. Some reservoirs are to store water. Some are to store food, as we do in our family welfare program and as Joseph did in the land of Egypt during the seven years of plenty. There should also be reservoirs of knowledge to meet the future needs; reservoirs of courage to overcome the floods of fear that put uncertainty in lives; reservoirs of physical strength to help us meet the frequent burdens of work and illness; reservoirs of goodness, reservoirs of stamina; reservoirs of faith. Yes, especially reservoirs of faith so that when the world presses in upon us, we stand firm and strong; when the temptations of a decaying world about us draw on our energies, sap our spiritual vitality, and seek to pull us down, we need a storage of faith that can carry youth and later adults over the dull, the difficult, the terrifying moments, disappointments, disillusionments, and years of adversity, want, confusion, and frustration. (Spencer W. Kimball, *Faith Precedes the Miracle* [Salt Lake City: Deseret Book Co., 1972], "Reservoirs of Righteousness," pp. 110-111.)

When I was a teenager, I rode with some friends from south Texas to northern Utah. In the middle of the west Texas desert, we ran out of gas. We were really worried about being stranded until a friend pointed out that the van we were driving in had a reserve gas tank. I cannot tell you how comforting it was, and easy, to be able to flip a switch and drive for 200 more miles.

I think that is the principle President Kimball was teaching us in his statement about reservoirs. But instead of a reserve tank of gas, we need to carry with us a "reserve tank" of spiritual food—knowledge, courage, strength, goodness, stamina, and faith. We are living in a time when Satan is rampant, violence has engulfed the world, immorality plagues communities, and morals are becoming extinct. Heber C. Kimball described our day this way:

> We think we are secure here in the chambers of the everlasting hills, where we can close those few doors of the canyons against the mobs and persecutors, the wicked and the vile, who have always beset us with violence and robbery, but I want to say to you, my brethren, the time is coming when we will be mixed up in these now peaceful valleys to the extent that it will be difficult to tell the face of a Saint from the face of an enemy to the people of God. Then brethren, look out for the great sieve, for there will be a great sifting time, and many will fall; for I say unto you there is a *test*, a TEST, a TEST coming, and who will be able to stand? (Orson F. Whitney, *Life of Heber C. Kimball* [Salt Lake City: Stevens and Wallis, Inc.], p. 446.)

Who will be able to stand? Brother Heber answered his own question when he later stated that "The time will come when no man nor woman will be able to endure on borrowed light. Each will have to be guided by the light within himself. If you do not have it, how can you stand?" *(Life of Heber C. Kimball*, pp. 449-450.) If we want to survive temporally and spiritually in these last days, we are going to need some extra gas in our tanks—or, to be more scriptural, oil in our lamps. We will not be able to rely on our neighbor's reserve supply; we will have to have our own surplus of faith, testimony, courage, and fortitude.

A PARABLE OF PREPARATION

In Matthew 25:1-13, we read one of the most important parables about how to prepare for the second coming of Christ—and really, about how to live the gospel daily. This parable tells the story of ten virgins, or maidens, who went to meet the groom. We learn that five of the maidens were wise, and five were foolish—foolish because they did not bring any reserve oil for their lamps. When evening came, all of the maidens fell asleep. Eventually, at midnight, the groom arrived and the maidens all lit their lamps. However, I suppose after some waiting, the lamps of the foolish maidens began to go out. In desperation, they asked the wise maidens if they could borrow some oil for their lamps. Of course, if the wise maidens shared their oil, they would not have enough for themselves; so the wise virgins instructed the foolish ones to go purchase some oil quickly. While they were out "shopping" for oil, the groom arrived and let all of the wise maidens into the house for the marriage festivities. I like the Greek translation of verse 10 because it teaches us that when the maidens returned, not only was the door shut, but it was locked, which suggests the finality of the situation. Moreover, when the foolish maidens begged the groom to let them in, he responded by saying, "I know you not." Those are hard words coming from the groom, especially when, as tradition suggests, he probably invited them to the wedding in the first place.

What can we learn about preparation from this parable? Thankfully, we have modern-day prophets who have given us some valuable insights. For example, from President Harold B. Lee we learn that the groom in this parable is Jesus Christ, the marriage feast is the second coming, and the ten virgins represent the membership of the Church today (see *Conference Report,* 1951, pp. 26-27). Furthermore, regarding the Church membership, Elder Wilford Woodruff stated the following:

> I expect that the Savior was about right when he said, in reference to the members of the Church, that five of them were wise and five were foolish; for when the Lord of heaven comes in power and great glory . . . , if he finds one-half of those professing to be members of his Church prepared for salvation, it will be as many as can be expected, judging by the course that many are pursuing. (Rulon T. Burton, *We Believe: Doctrines and Principles of The Church of Jesus Christ of Latter-day Saints,* [Salt Lake City: Tabernacle Books, 1994], pp. 942-943.)

So actually, this parable helps us understand that we'd better have oil in our lamps when Jesus comes, or we are going to be in big trouble. Banging on the "locked" front door of the celestial kingdom, for, let's say, eternity, and yelling "Let me in!" doesn't sound like the most exciting way to live out your life's existence.

Another symbol in this parable is the oil. What is the oil, and where do we get it? It appears to me that the oil represents obedience to the commandments. President Lee taught that

> The Lord gives us, each one, a lamp to carry, but whether or not we shall have oil in our lamps depends solely upon each one of us. Whether or not we keep the commandments and supply the needed oil to light our way and to guide us on our way depends upon each of us *individually.* We cannot borrow from our Church membership. We cannot borrow from an illustrious ancestry. Whether or not we have oil in our lamps, I repeat, *depends solely upon each one of us*, it is determined by our faithfulness in keeping the commandments of the living God. (Clyde J. Williams, *The Teachings of Harold B. Lee* [Salt Lake City: Bookcraft, 1996], pp. 145-146; emphasis added.)

Knowing that the oil represents obedience to the commandments, and that it is our responsibility, not anyone else's, to gain a testimony and live the gospel, Matthew 25:12 can be explained more adequately. Upon careful examination of that verse, we learn that Matthew 7:21-23 is an excellent cross-reference. These verses confirm what President Lee was alluding to—that it does not matter how well we have *pretended* to be a good follower of Christ. If we have not done the will of our Heavenly Father, then we have no claim to the celestial kingdom.

If we will prepare ourselves on a daily basis to be ready to meet the Savior when he comes again, then we will automatically be prepared for the smaller things that challenge us right now. I know that it is vital for us to prepare ourselves spiritually and temporally.

THE DOCTRINE OF PREPARATION

In the Doctrine and Covenants 38:30, the Lord states simply that "if ye are prepared ye shall not fear." To me, being prepared has always been a good idea; at least it could have saved some heartache on "Stinky Island." However, after reading the following statement by Elder Jeffrey R. Holland, I have changed my thinking somewhat. Not only is preparation a good idea, it is a *vital doctrine.* Consider Elder Holland's words:

> The Boy Scouts say it best of all: "Be Prepared." That isn't just cracker-barrel wisdom with us; it is theology. . . . The scriptures teach that preparation—prevention, if you will, is perhaps the major weapon in our arsenal against discouragement and self-defeat. (Jeffery R. Holland, *However Long and Hard the Road* [Salt Lake City: Deseret Book Co.], "For Times of Trouble," p. 3.)

In that same talk, Elder Holland quoted the late President John F. Kennedy, who said, "The time to repair the roof is when the sun is shining." I know the truth of that statement. I can still remember the time I tried to patch my roof in Mesa, Arizona, during a winter rainstorm. I was too late. The damage to the inside ceiling ended up costing much more than a gallon of roofing tar would have on a sunny day. For some reason, we mortals are not really keen on this notion of prevention. Many of us do not fix the roof until it leaks, water the grass until it's brown, or go to the doctor until we are sick. Why do we procrastinate prevention? Probably because it "costs" something to be prepared. The lesson to be learned, however, is that it *always* ends up costing much more when we are not prepared. My mother-in-law often observes that "An ounce of prevention is worth a pound of cure." I have learned the truth of that statement over the years. For example, it would have been much easier to put a drop cloth down on the floor before painting than to spend an entire afternoon scraping paint drops off the ceramic tile. Preventive maintenance is the solution to most of the difficulties we face.

SALVATION IN PREPARATION

Have you ever thought that your own preparation might actually save someone's life? Whether such a rescue could be physical or spiritual, I do not know. But I do know that we always need to be ready, because we never know when we might be called upon to help. Simply put, we never know when disaster is going to strike.

We need to be ready at all times—like BYU lineman Matt Meservey. One night, Matt couldn't sleep. He had suffered a concussion in a recent game, and at 2:30 a.m. he awoke with a severe headache and upset stomach. His head hurt too much to allow him to go back to sleep, so he decided to read an article in *Parents* magazine on how to save a baby from choking. Ten minutes later, he heard a faint noise from his sixteen-month-old son's room. Using the magazine article as his guide, Matt determined that little Jake was choking. He was shaking and had turned blue. Keri, Matt's wife, describes the scene:

> Matt rushed over and tried the baby Heimlich on him. That didn't work, so he felt in his throat for an obstruction. There was a small ball of cotton that he could barely reach in the back of Jake's throat. After several tries, he retrieved the ball of cotton and Jake was able to breathe again. . . . Doctor Darryl Stacy, the team physician, said if Matt had not been awake and heard the small sound and then removed the cotton, Jake would have died that night. (Keri Meservey, *Cougar Sports Magazine*, "Football and My Husband Saved the Life of My Son," December 12, 1995, vol. 3, no. 9, p. 26.)

I guess we never know how long after our preparation or practice we will be called upon to use our skills, knowledge, and talents. For some, it may be a lifetime; for Matt Meservey, it was ten minutes. Isn't it obvious why we always need to be worthy and ready to serve the Lord? If Matt hadn't been living a clean and pure life, I really doubt that he would have been receptive to the Holy Ghost, which prompted him into action that saved a life.

Recently, my brother-in-law, Marty Watkins, shared with a group of Eagle Scouts his testimony of the need to be prepared. Marty was snow skiing a few years ago, and broke his back in a freak accident. After he was rushed to the emergency room and the doctors consulted about their next course of action, Marty requested a blessing. Two men from a nearby ward were summoned and proceeded to give Marty the blessing he needed. Not only did they bless Marty that his back would heal, but that he would be able to go on his upcoming mission. It has been Marty's feeling that the only way he could pay back those two anonymous priesthood holders was to someday be able to return the favor for someone else. With emotion in his voice, Marty testified to those Eagle Scouts that night: "That day I decided that I would always be ready when called upon to give a priesthood blessing." I know Marty well, and I testify that he has done just that.

Elder Bruce R. McConkie declared: "Great trials lie ahead. All of the sorrows and perils of the past are but a foretaste of what is yet to be. And we must prepare ourselves temporally and spiritually" (*Ensign*, May 1979, p. 92). Being prepared is not merely a good idea, it is one of the most important and sacred doctrines our church teaches. We need to be ready for whatever lies ahead! I pray that we will.

Mark Ogletree *teaches at the Logan Institute and is a family counselor with LDS Social Services. He holds a bachelor's degree from Brigham Young University, a master's degree in counseling from Northern Arizona University, and is currently pursuing a doctorate in family and human development at Utah State University. Mark and his wife, Janie, are the parents of six children and live in Hyde Park, Utah, where he teaches the gospel doctrine class in his ward. He enjoys racquetball, softball, playing hide-and-seek with his children, remodeling houses, and jet skiing.*

9

THE FIRST VISION: MY WITNESS

Victor W. Harris

I can still remember the time I came to know for myself that Joseph Smith indeed saw God the Father and Jesus Christ in the theophany* we have all come to know as the "First Vision." I had just entered the Missionary Training Center en route to serving in the Switzerland Zurich Mission, and I was overwhelmed by trying to learn the discussions we would present to the Swiss people in their native language of German.

As I learned portions of the "First Vision" discussion in German, such as *"Wir möchten Ihnen sagen das Gott auch heute noch propheten auf der erde hat"* and *"...einer von Ihnen war Joseph Smith,"* I became concerned with a small English phrase at the end of the first section. It read, "Now bear your testimony about the fact that Joseph Smith saw God the Father and his son Jesus Christ."

I was cut to the heart with the feeling that I didn't really know for myself whether or not Joseph Smith had seen what he said he had witnessed in vision. Oh, I had gained a personal testimony of the Book of Mormon and the Church, but I wanted to know for myself

*A theophany is a visible manifestation of deity; in other words, a vision.

concerning Joseph's experience in the Sacred Grove. I also knew I could never tell people I knew this experience was true unless I really "knew" from God that it had happened. That very evening I began to plead for a personal testimony about the reality of the First Vision, realizing that this sacred event was the catalyst for the coming forth of the Book of Mormon and the restoration of the gospel.

I remember vividly when my witness came. We were attending a Swiss culture class on a Sunday evening about three weeks after my initial prayers concerning the First Vision began. In this class we learned such skills as proper eating and social etiquette. We were also warned about the tactics of elders out in the mission field who would try to amuse themselves at their younger and less experienced elders' ("greenies") expense.

For example, when an elder would take his greenie to get a haircut, the older elder ("trainer") might say, "Elder, you just tell the barber you want a *kaiserschnitt* today." Well, the word for "haircut" in German is *haarschnitt*. Both of these words sound similar, and an unsuspecting greenie might then say to the barber, "Just give me a *kaiserschnitt* today. The barber and the trainer would then burst out laughing. You see, a *kaiserscnitt* is a Cesarean section! Can you imagine the greenie saying, "Yes, just give me a C-section today!"

On other occasions, the trainers would dupe their younger companions into saying potentially disastrous phrases at dinner appointments. The Swiss and German women are, generally, very kind and very gratified during mealtimes when the elders show their appreciation for their cooking by asking for a second serving.

This is another occasion when an unscrupulous trainer can move in for the kill! First, he will simply tell his greenie to eat all that he can at their dinner engagement to show appreciation for the meal. When the *frau* or lady of the house offers him more food, the junior companion is to simply say: *Noch mehr, bitte*. This short phrase sounds like "No more, please," but in reality it means, "Still more, please." In other words, when the young elder is so stuffed he can hardly see straight, he utters these fateful words and the little *frau* smiles with glee as she fills his plate again with food!

During this particular culture class, the instructor had decided to show the movie version of the First Vision. I had seen this movie many times before, but I will never forget the light and warmth that filled my soul as I received my own personal witness. My heart burned as I observed Joseph behold God our Father and his Son Jesus Christ. My eyes filled with tears and my heart soared with gratitude as I thanked Heavenly Father for this sacred experience. I even cried through the funniest part, if you have seen the movie recently, when the little old lady at a revivalist movement cries out, "I believe!" In German it sounds even funnier as she cries, *"Ich habe Glauben!"*

I will be forever grateful for my witness of the First Vision. I testify to you, my young friends, that Joseph indeed saw God our Father and his Son and that this beautiful experience opened the heavens again in our day and paved the way for the restoration of the gospel.

I have a feeling that there are many aspects of the First Vision which can greatly benefit our lives and bless us, if we will let them. So first, before we focus on such aspects, let's see what you really know about the First Vision. What follows are nineteen questions about Joseph Smith's First Vision experience. As you read them, simply answer them as true or false in your mind.

1. Joseph had pondered his religious concerns since he was twelve.
2. When Joseph had read James 1:5, it was probably not the first time he had heard the scripture.
3. Joseph had never prayed vocally before.
4. Joseph went to a familiar wooded area that he had picked out before, which was near his father's farm, and prayed.
5. Joseph not only wanted to know which church to join, but he wanted to seek forgiveness of his sins and mourn over the sins of the world.
6. The evil power made Joseph's tongue seem swollen in his mouth so he couldn't speak.
7. Satan made unwanted and distracting thoughts go through Joseph's mind.
8. Joseph heard a noise behind him like someone walking towards him, so he jumped up and looked around, but saw nothing.
9. Joseph was just about to give up when he saw a pillar of light.

10. When the pillar of light reached the tops of the trees, the whole area around for some distance seemed to illuminate.
11. God the Father appeared first to Joseph Smith, then Jesus Christ appeared.
12. Jesus Christ said, "Joseph, my son, thy sins are forgiven thee."
13. Christ also said, "Behold, I am the Lord of glory; I was crucified for the world that all those who believe on my name may have eternal life."
14. God the Father and his Son exactly resembled each other in feature and likeness.
15. Joseph was told *twice* not to join any of the churches.
16. Even after Joseph Smith had received most of his revelations from the Lord, he was not able to tell of the many things that he had learned in his first vision.
17. Joseph also saw many angels in his vision.
18. After the vision, Joseph found himself lying on his back looking into heaven.
19. After this vision, Joseph was filled with love and for many days he rejoiced and knew that the Lord was with him. (Questions taken from Allen, James B. "Eight Contemporary Accounts of Joseph Smith's First Vision," *Improvement Era*, April 1970, pp. 4-13.)

So how do you think you did on this little quiz? Did you know that all nineteen questions are true? Pat yourself on the back and let's talk for a few moments about the significance of these truths in our lives.

1. Joseph had pondered his religious concerns since he was twelve.

Sooner or later this will happen to each one of us. We will begin to desire to know for ourselves whether or not the gospel is true and whether or not our lives are in harmony with gospel standards. On one occasion, several years ago, my son Mckay approached me and asked, "Dad, am I righteous?" I smiled and said, "Well, let's talk about what it means to be righteous."

As we finished our little discussion about righteousness, his heart was reassured as I said, "Yes, you are righteous."

As we ponder our religious concerns, Heavenly Father continues to feel after our hearts, reassuring us as we come to know him, "Yes, you are righteous."

2. *When Joseph read James 1:5, it was probably not the first time he had heard the scripture.*
3. *Joseph had never prayed vocally before.*
4. *Joseph went to a familiar wooded area that he had picked out before which was near his father's farm, and prayed.*
5. *Joseph not only wanted to know which church to join, but he also wanted to seek forgiveness of his sins and mourn over the sins of the world.*

"If any of you lack wisdom, let him ask of God . . ." was a common text in the revivalist sermons of Joseph's day. I find it profound that the ministers talked about asking God, but it took a young boy with childlike faith to break through the prayer barrier and unlock the heavens.

Where has our childlike faith gone? Do we still possess it? Can you remember when you were younger and you lost something and you pleaded with Heavenly Father in perfect faith to help you find it? Have some of us lost that childlike faith? Do we need to ask him to help us find that faith and hope which have been lost? I testify that we can find them again. I know we can. I also know that we can take all of our concerns to Heavenly Father, no matter how seemingly silly or serious, and that he will understand and help us. In our hearts, we intuitively know this is true, don't we?

I can still remember the first time I tried to pray vocally for fifteen minutes. Our priest quorum advisor, Brother Choate, had challenged us to pray for fifteen minutes and I figured it would be a breeze. As I knelt down by my bedside, my familiar place to pray, I prayed for everything I could think of and then looked at the clock. *Only thirty seconds* had passed. I could tell I was in trouble so I shifted into Brother Choate's Plan B option and took the next hour to write down all of the things I could think of to pray for. I used this sheet during my prayers for the next few weeks, gradually needing it less and less.

Now, I'm not suggesting that fifteen minutes is the magical time period that helps us to break through in prayer to Heavenly Father, but I want you to know that I began to receive great strength and comfort from my prayers.

Think for a moment, if you would, about your best friends and how much time you spend with these people each day. If you never saw these people again, never talked with them again, and never thought about them again, what kind of relationship would you have with them? So it is with Heavenly Father. If we want to feel close to him, we must spend a regular amount of time talking with and thinking about him.

As I began to spend more time on my knees, I began to realize my intense desire to be forgiven of my sins and to be clean. It is such a great experience to be forgiven and to be guilt-free!

Joseph gives us a grand key to obtaining the spirit and spiritual experiences. Do you know what it is? Seek first to be forgiven and to become clean, and then beautiful spirit-filled experiences will follow. I know this is true.

6. *The evil power made Joseph's tongue seem swollen in his mouth so he couldn't speak.*
7. *Satan made unwanted and distracting thoughts go through Joseph's mind.*
8. *Joseph heard a noise behind him like someone walking towards him, so he jumped up and looked around, but saw nothing.*
9. *Joseph was just about to give up when he saw the pillar of light.*
10. *When the pillar of light reached the tops of the trees, the whole area around for some distance seemed to illuminate.*

The devil is real, alive, and bent on our destruction. From Joseph's experience we learn that the source of unwanted, judgmental, immoral, and distracting thoughts is Satan, for God would never tolerate such thoughts. However, we must realize that although we are constantly bombarded with such thoughts, sinful thoughts only occur when we allow them to act and play on the stages of our minds. I believe the battleground for the celestial kingdom is in the mind. If we will refuse to tolerate rude, judgmental, immoral, lustful thoughts, then these thoughts will never become a part of our emotions or behavior. It was Benjamin Franklin who said, "'Tis easier to suppress the first desire than to satisfy all that follows it."

From Joseph we also learn never to give up during our greatest times of trial and darkness. As one popular musical artist said it: "Hold on, the light will come."

11. *God the Father appeared first to Joseph Smith, then Jesus Christ appeared.*
12. *Jesus Christ said, "Joseph, my son, thy sins are forgiven thee."*
13. *Christ also said, "Behold, I am the Lord of glory. I was crucified for the world that all those who believe on my name may have eternal life."*
14. *God the Father and his son resembled each other exactly in feature and likeness.*

In this vision, Joseph learned some marvelous truths. One such truth was that Joseph was audibly told he was forgiven. Wouldn't that be wonderful? Most of us probably won't be blessed to experience forgiveness in this manner, but we can still have the blessing of forgiveness. Do you know how we, too, can know that we are forgiven? I have learned that this reassurance of forgiveness comes through the sweet peace of the Holy Ghost. The Holy Ghost cannot dwell in unclean tabernacles. Therefore, if we can obtain the Holy Ghost in our prayers of repentance, we can begin to know that we are being forgiven.

Another significant truth Joseph learned while in the Sacred Grove was that Heavenly Father and Jesus Christ look very much alike. When I pray and desire to create a mental picture of Heavenly Father in my mind, I have become accustomed to choosing my favorite picture of Jesus, imagining him with white hair, and then visualizing that this individual is Heavenly Father.

15. *Joseph was told twice not to join any of the churches.*
16. *Even after Joseph Smith had received most of his revelations from the Lord, he was not able to tell of the many things that he had learned in his first vision.*

17. *Joseph saw many angels in his vision.*
18. *After the vision, Joseph found himself lying on his back looking into heaven.*
19. *After this vision, he was filled with love and for many days he rejoiced and knew that the Lord was with him.*

I testify that, as Joseph learned for himself, this church is true. It not only makes sense in our minds, but also in our hearts, doesn't it? Think about all that we have and enjoy because of this true and living church restored through Joseph. We have temples, priesthood power, the knowledge of the spirit world and the life beyond, the Book of Mormon, the Doctrine & Covenants, the Pearl of Great Price, the Joseph Smith Translation, living prophets, the three degrees of glory, the sealing power and the hope of forever families, and even more.

The appearance of angels and their ministry is another beautiful truth restored through the First Vision. Joseph saw and was tutored by many angels during his lifetime among whom were Adam, Eve, Seth, Enoch, Noah, Abraham, Isaac, Jacob, Moses, Elias, Elijah, John the Baptist, Peter, James, John, Nephi, Alma, the three Nephites, Mormon, Moroni, and Paul.

After the First Vision, Joseph found himself lying on his back on the ground, exhausted. Can you remember times when you have felt physically exhausted after having had a spiritual experience? After this sacred vision, Joseph was also filled with love and knew that the Lord was with him. I hunger and thirst to be filled with this love. I live for this feeling! Doesn't it feel wonderful to know that the Lord is with us?

Over the years, I have been asked how a person can know whether or not a dream (or a vision) has come from God or whether or not it simply originated from the mind's psychological processes. My answer has always been that the Lord holds himself responsible to let us know that the dream has come from him. One of the ways he witnesses to us that our dream is divine is by filling us with his love. It is this love, his love, that brings me and my loved ones such joy and peace. I want you, my young friends, to know that I love this gospel with all of my heart. I know God lives. I know Jesus Christ is the Son of God. I know that this church and the Book of Mormon are true, and I know and testify to you that God the Father and his Son Jesus Christ appeared to Joseph Smith in the Sacred Grove. I testify further that we can come to know and understand the truths taught to Joseph in the First Vision, and these truths have the power to return us to live with our Father in Heaven again.

A seminary teacher in Logan, Utah, ***Victor W. Harris*** *graduated in psychology from Brigham Young University and is currently working toward a master's degree in marriage and family relations. While at Brigham Young University he performed with the Young Ambassadors and with U.S.O. groups. He enjoys tennis, basketball, wrestling, and writing music, and has just completed his first music CD, "Be Not Afraid." Victor and his wife, Heidi, have three children.*

10

Hands That Help

Lisa Heckmann Olsen

John was a twenty-year-old high school senior. He was bigger than all the rest of the students in my art class, and he was handicapped. Students whispered about him during class, quietly making fun of his disabilities. He was oblivious to the words, but I still wanted to protect him from their cruel comments, so I changed his seat to share my teacher's desk.

During the semester, we studied Indian pottery and made beautiful black shiny pots. John loved his pot, and he came to class early and left late so he could work on it as much as possible. He was very proud of his creation when he finally presented it to be graded. I looked at his grinning face, then I looked at the pot. It was funny looking, lopsided, with uneven thick and thin walls and its design carved crookedly. The glaze, applied awkwardly, had formed huge glass beads at the base of the pot. But I knew that he had worked harder than anyone, so when he asked me to write his grade in permanent pen on the bottom of the pot, I did: "100/100 A." John was ecstatic, and anxious to show the pot to his mother.

One boy in the class noticed our interaction. He grabbed some clay, quickly formed a terrible-looking pot, and brought it up to me. Dropping the shapeless form on my desk, he sneered, "Heckmann, grade my pot!" I told him I wouldn't grade an incomplete project. He responded quickly, "But you graded John's, and he's got an ugly pot!" John was sitting at the corner of the desk and heard the conversation. It made me sad that he had to hear things like this daily.

A few days later, John's medication was changed. It made him very tired in class. After waking him up three times, I finally gave up and let him sleep. When I turned my back to help another student, someone yelled, "Miss Heckmann, something's wrong with John!" John was shaking uncontrollably in a seizure. A couple of the strong boys in class helped me pull him down to the floor; we held his big, awkward body tight and close to the ground so he wouldn't hurt himself on the cement. When the seizure was over, he fell asleep, exhausted.

As the students stood around John, shocked at what they had witnessed, I could tell they felt terrible. They went to another classroom so John wouldn't be embarrassed when he woke up. I joined them a few minutes later, and we talked about seizures and John's situation. I wanted to pull out my Book of Mormon, tell the students to repent, and talk about how we should treat others. Unfortunately, in a public school setting I couldn't do that sort of thing; but we still talked about how John had been treated and what we could do to make life easier for him. The students worked hard the rest of the semester to help him and to be his friend, but I always felt bad that it took such a dramatic event to get them to offer a hand. These students had been "compelled to serve" (D&C 58:26).

Like John, each teenager has a unique set of problems and challenges. If you have ever had the feeling that your life isn't all you want it to be, my suggestion is that you change your entire focus. The Savior invited us to "lose our lives" for his sake in order to find our lives (Mark 8:35). This suggests that if you want to put your problems into perspective, you need to consider someone other than yourself. Lose your life. To start, love and serve ***one*** person. As we honor our covenants to follow Christ's example of service, our own lives will be blessed.

SERVICE: THE EXAMPLE

As I picture the Savior, images of helping people come to my mind.

The Savior lived a caring and compassionate life. Among his closest friends were two sisters, Mary and Martha, to whom he showed great respect and love. He ate at their home and talked with them about the gospel (Luke 10:38-42). When their brother Lazarus died, the Savior came to comfort them. When he arrived, he did not immediately go about raising Lazarus from the dead (which would certainly have been the most spectacular scenario). Instead, he sought out the family, and "he wept" with them (John 11:35). Friends and family loved the Savior because they knew he loved each of them, including Lazarus. After mourning with the family, he went to Lazarus's tomb and used his priesthood power to raise him from the dead.

Every example of the Savior's perfect life involved another soul. Because Christ's mission, along with that of his Father, has always been to "bring to pass the immortality and eternal life of man" (Moses 1:39), his life was never focused on selfish personal needs, but exactly the opposite: he put others' needs first. Elder Neal A. Maxwell wrote, "Jesus loved us enough to put His own needs in the background in order to better serve others. There was no selfishness about Him, nor any of the "I must meet my needs" philosophy that has seduced and captured so many in our time. Just as He has told us to do, He found and fulfilled Himself by losing Himself in the service of others. But we must lose our life for His sake—not just any cause" (*All These Things Shall Give Thee Experience* [Salt Lake City: Deseret Book Co., 1980], pp.68-69).

While serving a mission, I came close to completely "losing my life" for the Savior's sake. Even so, I often felt like an "unprofitable servant" (Mosiah 2:21) because I always felt so deeply rewarded for what I was doing.

Christine was the perfect investigator. She constantly put others' needs ahead of her own. Sister Robertson and I knocked at her door on May 4, 1987, in Marseille, France. When she answered, I saw a petite French girl with short, stylish black hair and huge dark eyes. She stared straight at us and said (before we had a chance to talk), "You're the Mormon missionaries—I prayed you here!" I was surprised by this statement. She invited us in, and we taught her the first discussion. In the course of the lesson, we learned that she had been studying with the Jehovah's Witnesses, but didn't feel right about joining them and prayed to meet some Mormons (WOW!!). Christine had lived a difficult and traumatic life. A month previous to our visit, she had tried to commit suicide. As a result, life had become her most precious possession. Her father had taken his own life when she was thirteen. She continued to struggle with the loss over the next six years and became addicted to the tranquilizers that were intended to help her cope. She was also a chain smoker.

"At the end of the discussion, we prayed together. I asked God to bless Christine with all of her struggles and to bless her while she read the Book of Mormon. After the prayer she just sat there. Her eyes were BIG. Not a word came out of her mouth. Then she just looked at me. 'I didn't think anyone loved me,' she said, 'but now I know someone does' (implying God). She continued, 'I feel like I want to cry.' But by then I was already bawling. She started to cry too. 'I have never felt so good in my life!'" (Excerpt from mission journal, volume 8, p. 192.)

As we learned more about Christine's addictions and struggles, I knew that it would be a long road to baptism. I thought often of the Savior and "how he healed the sick physically first; then he healed them spiritually" (Journal, p. 227). We suggested that she enroll in a drug rehabilitation program, and offered to teach her while she was there.

Christine had more problems than any person I have ever met. She had a right to complain about her life, but just like Job, she praised the name of God instead (see Job 1:21). Her secret to finding happiness was thinking of others before herself.

When we taught her the second discussion, Christine insisted that her sister listen too. At the third discussion, she had a list of referrals for us. She was a full-time nonmember missionary! She talked to strangers, told them that she was going to be a Mormon, and challenged them to be one too. Surprisingly, they wanted to know more.

Christine needed surgery on her jaw, and she was frightened. She asked if we could come with the elders the day before the surgery to give her a blessing. When we arrived at l'Hospital Timone, we found her in a room she shared with six other people. She was lying on her bed, reading from the Book of Mormon we had given her. "This is the only thing that could bring me peace," she said. The nurses allowed us to meet in a tiny operating room, which made Christine even more nervous. She sat in a chair and asked me to sit by her and hold her hand. Elder Manne, a French elder, promised her peace, comfort, and health in the blessing. I could feel her tears on my hands. After the blessing, the Spirit was stronger than I had ever felt it before. Christine, the investigator, said to me, "You're feeling the Spirit—everything's going to be okay!" My goal was to help Christine, but in the process she had taught me, lifted me, blessed my life.

The next day, we returned to an awful sight. Christine was half awake, her arms and legs twisted and crippled, her mouth open, head back, and eyes rolled back in their sockets. We panicked when she insisted that we leave. We laid a beautiful long-stemmed rose next to her tiny sick body, then ran through the hospital looking for her boyfriend. Bruno explained that she was so frightened that they had called off the surgery. The day before, she had been taken off tranquilizers and couldn't smoke, and now she was experiencing severe depression and muscle spasms. She was a mess.

She looked better the next day, but she was concerned about one thing. "See the lady next to me?" Christine said that she had been in a car accident and was all alone. Christine told her about the Book of Mormon and taught her how to pray. "I gave her the rose because she needed it more than I did. Are you mad at me?" Sister Robertson and I just cried. She was amazing to us because she never thought about herself—only others.

This all happened during the last month of my mission. When Christine left for Denmark to receive treatment in a better drug rehabilitation clinic, she promised to keep in touch with the missionaries so she could eventually be baptized. It broke my heart when we lost contact with her.

SERVICE: THE COVENANT (MORE THAN JUST A GOOD IDEA)

As a missionary, I often shared the passages in Mosiah 18 concerning baptism. Prior to the baptisms in the waters of Mormon, wicked King Noah ordered the prophet Abinadi to be burned for his belief in God and Christ. Alma heard Abinadi's testimony and knew the gospel was true; he "repented of his sins and iniquities, and went about privately among the people, and began to teach the words of Abinadi" (Mosiah 18:1). Alma had to teach in secret, because King Noah punished those like Abinadi who talked about God. But the believers found a secret gathering place in Mormon where "wild beasts" roamed from time to time and the waters were hidden in a thicket of trees (Mosiah 18:3-5). Here they felt safe. Alma invited the believers to be baptized, and explained the covenant of service: ". . . as ye are desirous to come into the fold of God, and to be called his people, and are willing to bear one another's burdens, that they may be light; Yea, and are willing to mourn with those that mourn; yea, and comfort those that stand in need of comfort . . ."(Mosiah 18:8-9). He also explained other covenants and promised that if they were kept, the Lord would "pour out his Spirit more abundantly" upon them (Mosiah 18:10).

When we enter into the covenant of baptism, we take upon us the name of Christ. This means that we promise to help him fulfill his purpose, also God's purpose, which is "to bring to pass the immortality and eternal life of man" (Moses 1:39). This is done through serving others.

The Prophet Joseph Smith shared his time, his talents, his money, and anything else he could give to help others. Andrew Workman recalled that Joseph was talking to a group of men one day when "a man came up and said that a poor brother who lived out some distance from town had had his house burned down the night before. Nearly all of the men said they felt sorry for the man. Joseph put his hand in his pocket, took out five dollars and said, 'I feel sorry for this brother to the amount of five dollars; how much do you all feel sorry?'" (*Ensign*, June 1994, p. 14).

Sometimes the Prophet sacrificed time. On one occasion Joseph wrote, "The store has been filled to overflowing and I have stood behind the counter all day, distributing goods as steadily as any clerk you ever saw, to oblige those who were compelled to go without their Christmas and New Year's dinners for the want of a little sugar, molasses, raisins, etc.; and to please myself also, for I love to wait upon the Saints and to be a servant to all, hoping that I may be exalted in the due time of the Lord" (*BYU 1986-1987 Devotional and Fireside Speeches,* Howard W. Hunter, p. 113). The last phrase worries me and makes me want to serve more. If the Prophet was *hoping* to be exalted, I have a lot of work to do!

SERVICE: THE REWARD

The Lord would never ask us to do anything that doesn't benefit us. Naturally, service blesses the lives of those we help; but it eventually comes back to bless the giver, as well.

Joseph and Emma Smith served, sacrificed, and shared. Through it all, Joseph always had faith that the Lord would provide for their needs if they continued to think of others first. Because they prepared so many meals for travelers, Saints, or visitors, "There were times when the cupboard was bare. One day they had nothing to eat but a little corn meal. They made out of it a johnnycake, as it was called, and the Prophet offered the blessing as follows: 'Lord, we thank thee for this johnnycake and ask thee to send us something better. Amen.' Before the meal was over a knock came at the door, and there stood a man with a ham and some flour. The Prophet jumped to his feet and said to Emma, 'I knew the Lord would answer my prayer.' He shared and shared until he was utterly impoverished" (Truman G. Madsen, *Joseph Smith the Prophet* [Salt Lake City: Bookcraft, 1989], p. 31). Like the example of the Prophet, I know the Lord will bless us in proportion to how generous we are when we serve.

One of the greatest blessings of service is that the change of focus it requires puts our own problems into perspective. No matter how rotten or terrible we believe our plight in life to be, there will always be someone who has a more difficult load to carry. As we reach out to these others, our personal load will seem lighter and the Lord will provide "rest unto our souls" (Matthew 11:29). "To lose yourself in righteous service to others can lift your sights and get your mind off personal problems, or at least put them in proper focus. 'When you find yourselves a little gloomy,' said President Lorenzo Snow, 'look around you and find somebody that is in a worse plight than yourself; go to him and find out what the trouble is, then try to remove it with the wisdom which the Lord bestows upon you; and the first thing you know, your gloom is gone, you feel light, the Spirit of the Lord is upon you, and everything seems illuminated'" (*Conference Report,* April 6, 1899, pp. 2-3).

As a result of serving a full-time mission, I received incredible blessings: my testimony grew stronger, my talents developed, my ability to work with people was enhanced, and more. But the blessings didn't end with the last day of my mission. One reward came six years later in the form of a letter. Now to finish a great story.

When my husband Brent and I were married, I sent a wedding invitation to Christine's old address with the hope that someone would forward it to her. One year later I received a long letter from her, describing in detail the events of her life since her experience in Denmark. She came home drug-free, but she had lost all interest in the Church. She went to college and became a dance instructor, then she entered a beauty pageant and was named "Miss Marseille." She had a great new boyfriend, Jean-Pierre, and life was good. But then she was in a moped accident and damaged her legs so severely that her employer asked her to quit her dance teaching job. (She could still walk, but her mobility was limited). At the age of twenty-five, she was forced to work at McDonald's to have money to pay her bills.

One day she was walking on La Cannonbiere, the main road of town, and saw two missionaries. All the feelings about the gospel came rushing back to her. She ran up to the elders and said, "I need to be baptized!" I can only imagine the shocked reaction of the two elders. Christine received all the missionary discussions for the second time, and two months later was baptized. When I read about her baptism, I cried and cried. (My husband wondered what tragedy would make me so emotional.) She thanked me over and over again for coming to France to share the gospel. As a result of the baptism, her family had rejected her, but she was happy because now she enjoyed the full blessings of the gospel.

Late one evening, she was walking home alone and had to pass through a bad neighborhood. Petite Christine lacked protection and was attacked by five men. They went through her bag, stealing her money and other possessions before coming across the Book of Mormon we had given her six years earlier. She carried it with her wherever she went. When these men realized that she was a Mormon, they took a permanent black marker from her purse and wrote "Mormon" over her arms and face. Then they took her Book of Mormon and ran. Christine went straight to her bishop's home because she had nowhere else to go. The bishop took her to the police, and with her testimony they were able to capture and punish the men. Sadly, she never recovered her original Book of Mormon; that was the thing that upset her most about the entire incident.

Christine closed the letter with her testimony, and, still true to her loving nature, her last sentence read, "Lisa, I'm still going to church. Are you?" Once again, this special young woman was concerned about someone else. (We have continued to stay in touch.)

SERVICE: THE CHALLENGE

I love the story of the shepherd with 100 sheep, one of which goes astray (Luke 15:4). It not only illustrates the love the Savior has for his children who stray, but also shows that he loves each of God's children. I also love the story of the resurrected Savior allowing 2,500 people to touch the nail marks in his hands and feet as a uniquely personal testimony of his mission and sacrifice. Each person is important to Christ (see 3 Nephi 11:15). We may not be able to touch the lives of 2,500 people at once, but we can certainly touch one person's life.

Just think about it: Last year, 920 boys attended Boys World of Adventure; over 18,000 teenagers came to EFY; and 1,940 young women participated in Academy for Girls. That makes a grand total of 20,860 teenagers. The challenge is this: Choose ***one*** person. Just one. During this coming year, work to lift this person and make his or her life easier. At the end of the year, more than 41,720 lives will be affected. What? I can't add? (I'm an art teacher, not a math teacher, I deserve a break . . .) Where did I get 41,720? Here's the thing: Not only will the life of the person you serve change, but I know that *your* life will change, too. Just think of the prospect: 41,720 happier teenage lives! Wonderful!

Now, don't just close this book and say, "Well, Lisa had a nice idea." ACT ON IT! DO IT! DON'T JUST THINK ABOUT IT AND WAIT FOR SOMEONE ELSE TO DO IT! Two years ago at a special fireside, I listened to President Howard W. Hunter testify of the power of service. He said one thing that I memorized instantly: "Hands that help are more sacred than lips that pray." President Hunter's word are true. As we use our hands to help, and stop praying for a change, our own lives will be blessed and the necessary change will occur.

I know that God loves each one of his children, and that he depends on us to take our covenant of service seriously so that all can feel his love. Lend a pair of hands that help, and be a part of God's plan for the blessing of his children.

Lisa Heckmann Olsen *teaches and serves as the student government adviser at Timpview High School in Utah. She served a mission in Geneva, Switzerland, and has worked for several years in the EFY program. She loves painting, gardening, making stained glass, and playing with her pet snake, Rachid. Lisa and her husband, Brent, have one son, Cole.*

11

Feasting on the Scriptures: That Delicious, Delectable Desirable Diet

Mark Ellison

Imagine that you invited me to your home for Thanksgiving dinner, and you set out a real feast for me to enjoy: hot, juicy roast turkey; creamy mashed potatoes covered with melted butter and rich gravy; stuffing and yams, corn and rolls; frosty goblets of chilled sparkling cider—in short, a spectacular spread. After a prayer of thanks over the meal, you would say, "Let's eat!" Then, what if all I took was a spoonful of whipped cream off the top of the pumpkin pie?

"Hey," you'd begin to say with difficulty due to the roll in your mouth, "Thith ith delithious—try thome."

"Nah," I shrug, my mouth full of froth. "I juth like thweets."

"You just like *sweets?"* Now you would protest: "It took a long time to prepare this meal! Come on, I know you'll love the dressing if you'll just have a taste. You're missing out! Eat some turkey, you turkey."

"Doesn't sound interesting," I reply lamely. How would you feel?

Taking this a bit further, how might the Lord feel when his children fail to enjoy the "feast" provided for them in the scriptures? The

Bible, Book of Mormon, Doctrine and Covenants, and Pearl of Great Price have been prepared over centuries, with innumerable hours—even lifetimes—of work devoted to their compilation. People have sacrificed their lives to translate, keep, or protect these sacred records, and God has literally worked miracles so that we might have them. "Never before in any dispensation have the Saints been so abundantly blessed with the words of the Lord and His prophets" (Ezra Taft Benson, *Ensign*, May 1984, p. 7).

What if our scriptures remain closed day after day while our eyes are glued to the TV? Or what if stake dances, ward basketball games, activities, or other "sweets" are the extent of our involvement in the Church? If that's all we partake of, we're definitely missing out! And, worse, we're spiritually starving ourselves. The Lord counsels: "Do not spend money for that which is of no worth, nor your labor for that which cannot satisfy. . . . come unto the Holy One of Israel, and *feast* upon that which perisheth not, neither can be corrupted, and let your soul delight in fatness" (2 Nephi 9:51; emphasis added).

BLESSINGS OF FEASTING

God promises great blessings to those who feast on his words. 2 Nephi 31:20 tells us, "If ye shall press forward, feasting upon the word of Christ, and endure to the end, behold, thus saith the Father: *Ye shall have eternal life*" (emphasis added). A few verses later, we're told to "Feast upon the words of Christ; for behold, *the words of Christ will tell you all things what ye should do*" (2 Nephi 32:3; emphasis added). Think about how important those blessings are: The words of Christ help us endure righteously in this life, tell us all things that we should do here, and guide us safely back to our Father.

When you take a test at school and your teacher says you may use your textbook, you don't just leave it under your desk. You practically wear it out flipping through the pages, searching for answers! That textbook tells you "all things what ye should do" on the test; it helps you get an A. Likewise, this life is a test—thank goodness it's an open-book test!

Nephi turned to the scriptures to face the tests of his life. Did you notice how each of the "feasting" verses I just quoted came from the writings of this great prophet? He *loved* the scriptures. He willingly retraced his steps hundreds of miles across the desert, facing hardships and even death threats, to retrieve the brass plates—because "they were *desirable;* yea, even of *great worth*" (1 Nephi 5:21; emphasis added). When he met obstacles, he took courage by remembering stories from his scriptures (see 1 Nephi 4:2-3, 17:23-51). He wrote about how a sacred book affected his father, Lehi: "And it came to pass that *as he read, he was filled with the Spirit of the Lord*" (1 Nephi 1:12; emphasis added). Nephi himself *delighted* in what he read (2 Nephi 25:5), and because the scriptures persuade people to believe in Christ, he loved to read them to his family (see 1 Nephi 19:22-24). When Nephi tells us about the blessings of scriptural feasting, he's speaking from experience!

"THE SCRIPTURES ARE BORING," AND OTHER LIES

I once had a seminary student who refused to open his scriptures or participate in class. Instead, he would put his head down and go to sleep. "The scriptures are boring," was his attitude. I found out that his best friend had just died. In his depression, he was turning to the world for escape instead of turning to God for comfort. Ignoring encouragement from me, his parents, his bishop, and his friends, he continued to make choices that sent his life into a downward spiral. He dropped out of seminary, leaving his scriptures behind. When I found them, I leafed through the crisp, unmarked, unread pages of his Book of Mormon. On its own, it fell open to page 71, and the first verse my eyes rested on was 2 Nephi 8:12: "I am he; yea, *I am he that comforteth you.*" I ached inside, as if I was not the one who was meant to have read that verse. I wondered: What if my student, just once, had opened his Book of Mormon? Would he have discovered that verse? What would it have meant to him, his heart breaking with sadness, to have read, "I am he that comforteth you"? Would those have been just the words he needed? Maybe he would have found the powerful peace that only God can give (see Jacob 2:8). I have hope that someday he will, for the end of his story isn't written yet.

There is someone who wants you to think the scriptures are boring. He is your enemy, and he "seeketh that all men might be miserable like unto himself" (2 Nephi 2:27). He knows that if he can get you to *despise* the scriptures (meaning to look down on them, or to think they're boring or of little value), you will miss out on their spiritual power and be more likely to come under his power. "Whoso despiseth the word shall be destroyed" (Proverbs 13:13); "Wherefore, brethren, despise not the revelations of God" (Jacob 4:8).

GREATER SPIRITUALITY

A young woman I know escaped being "destroyed" because she learned to "despise not the revelations of God" and turned to the scriptures for personal help. I met this girl at a youth conference I visited. She was especially fun to talk with because of her quick wit and pleasant personality. I was surprised when she told me that she'd had a long habit of drug abuse. She had been clean for two months, she said, and this youth conference was the first time in years she'd been to a church function. "But everyone has been so friendly and wonderful!" she remarked. "I feel like I've come home." The weekend was a great boost for her. A couple of months later, she honored me with a letter. I'd like to share part of it here, pointing out that the Holy Spirit was a key part of her recovery, and the scriptures were a key to inviting the Spirit into her life:

> Every day I grow stronger and learn more. I'm so excited about life now! I'm getting closer to my Heavenly Father, which is so great. I've never felt this way.
>
> I just got back from Education Week at BYU. I'm on a total spiritual high and hope I can always walk with the Spirit. So many great things have happened to me since Youth Conference. I'm learning a lot about prayer, and how important the scriptures are.
>
> I've begun to read the Book of Mormon, and am gaining a stronger testimony.
>
> Tomorrow I am going to High School for the first time sober. The first day of school is always scary for me. It's gonna be hard to be around all those other kids I used to hang with, and have to tell them I really don't have the strength to hang

> with them and stand up for my values at the same time. That would be hard for anyone. . . . It's gonna be hard, but one scripture keeps going through my mind—1 Nephi 3:7: "I will go and do the things which the Lord commandeth."
>
> There's so much in store!

This young woman's experience illustrates what President Ezra Taft Benson once said: "More than at any time in our history we have need for greater spirituality. The way to develop greater spirituality is to feast on the words of Christ as revealed in the scriptures" *(Ensign*, May 1984, p. 7). *Greater spirituality.* This is what makes scripture reading a feast—it opens the way for the Spirit to feed us, to personally teach us and strengthen us (see *Ensign*, January 1995, pp. 7-9).

LOOKING TO LIKEN

Notice, also, that my youth conference friend discovered the value of the scriptures when she applied them to her own life. Nephi sought the brass plates long ago in a distant land, but this girl found a lesson in that story which would help her 2,600 years later, on her first sober day of high school. Nephi himself tells us about this method of scripture study: *"I did liken all scriptures unto us*, that it might be for our profit and learning" (1 Ne. 19:23). Look for the principles behind the stories, and apply those principles to your life. "Find yourself in the scriptures," a *New Era* article explains:

> In the story of Zaccheus (Luke 19:2-8), is that little man up there in the sycamore tree really you? Is the Lord trying to get your attention? In the story of the prodigal son (Luke 15:11-32), are you the "good" brother? And have you come to realize that you are the wayward brother—along with everyone else in the world? (*The New Era*, July 1991, p. 17.)

SCRIPTURAL FEASTING IS A TALENT

As you learn to liken the scriptures to yourself, remember that learning from the scriptures is a talent. Picture a young man who wants to make the basketball team. He gets up early to work out before school, and he stays late to practice after school. He lifts weights and runs a mile a day. He watches his favorite NBA players and tries to imitate their moves. He shoots baskets in the driveway late at night until his mom calls him in. Now, you would call that dedication—hard work!—and you would tell me that hard work will eventually pay off for that young man. "To become good at something, you have to pay a price," you'd say. And you would be right.

Yet, I know of LDS young people who will scan a few verses of scripture (perhaps late at night or while listening to the radio), close the book, set it aside, and then wonder why they don't get much out of their reading. Elder Bruce R. McConkie said that people "will be denied the sweet whisperings of the Spirit that might have been theirs unless they *pay the price of studying, pondering,* and *praying* about the scriptures" (*Ensign*, May 1986, p. 81; emphasis added). We get out of things about what we put into them (see Galatians 6:7-9, 2 Corinthians 9:6). It's not like TV, where you don't need to think; with the scriptures, you'll need to go digging. It will take time. But as with any talent—basketball, dancing, piano—effort pays off, bringing great joy. I know young people who have amazing wisdom and scriptural insights, who have let daily scripture study give them rock-solid faithfulness. Some have been my students, although it would be more accurate to say that, at times, they have been my teachers.

Some people have more difficulty reading than others, and must struggle to develop the talent to feast on the scriptures. One such person impressed me by how she handled that challenge. Hilarie Cole told her story in the General Young Women's meeting on March 25, 1995:

> Because of my learning disability, it was hard to read the words [in the scriptures] and even more difficult to understand them. I often felt embarrassed and frustrated. I didn't like to go to Young Women because I felt inadequate. I was afraid I might be called on to read. . . . I prayed for help and I found this scripture. . . . "And Christ hath said: If ye will

> have faith in me ye shall have power to do whatsoever thing is expedient in me" [Moroni 7:33]. What a wonderful promise! If I would put my faith in the Lord, he would help me. . . . One verse at a time, one day at a time, I began to understand. Even my schoolwork improved. The Book of Mormon got me through high school. (The *Ensign*, May 1995, p. 95.)

FEASTING WITH FRIENDS

One time, a student of mine named Lori challenged me to a race. We both wanted to read the entire Book of Mormon during the summer before school started. "I bet I finish before you," I kidded. "Well, well!" she said, "I rather think not." Or something like that. We made an agreement (a nice way of saying we made a bet): If I finished first, Lori would baby-sit my kids for free one evening so my wife and I could go out on a fun date together. If Lori finished first, my wife and I would host a group date for Lori and her friends, cooking and serving them a nice Italian dinner. The race was on.

Every day, we would check our progress:

"Where are you?"

"Third Nephi."

"No, you're not!"

"I meant Second Nephi. Where are you?"

"Alma! Nanner nanner." It was great motivation!

A few days later: "Where are you now?"

"Helaman 24."

"No way—there is no Helaman 24!"

"I meant Mosiah 24. Just testing you. Where are you?"

"Alma. Still Alma."

I found there was much to be learned from a quick reading of the Book of Mormon, rather than my typical slow, deliberative reading. I gained an understanding of the Book of Mormon in overview; I saw grand themes repeated through the generations; I noticed differences in each writer's style; I felt its massive spiritual power. And I fell more deeply in love with the book.

I was in Moroni 7 when I got a phone call from Lori. "Brother Ellison," she said, "guess what I just did?"

"What?"

"Finished Moroni 10!" So Sister Ellison and I hosted a little Italian dinner for six. I've never enjoyed losing so much. I, too, had a feast.

Friends can be a great source of motivation to read. I know of young people who get together as groups of friends from time to time, just to read the scriptures. I've read about Book of Mormon marathon reading slumber parties. I know that I personally get much more out of the scriptures when I read them with my wife. We'll sit at our kitchen table together, reading and sharing insights, with colored pencils and pens handy to mark things we discover. "A kind of spiritual fire is lit when reverent people share thoughts and feelings about the scriptures" (*New Era*, July 1991, p. 18).

LIKE THE LIAHONA

During that "race" with Lori, I used a brand new, unmarked paperback Book of Mormon. My regular scriptures are filled with markings—notes in the margins, underlinings, arrows and lines connecting thoughts on the page, Post-it notes with quotes or diagrams on them. But that summer I wanted a fresh, new reading of the Book of Mormon. As I read, I found things I had never noticed before—exciting discoveries, verses that amazed me, answers to my prayers. "Why didn't I see that before?" I kept asking myself.

I found out that the scriptures are a little like the Liahona (see Alma 37:38-45). The Liahona was the ball, or compass, that directed Lehi and his family to the promised land. It worked according to the faith and diligence and heed Lehi's family gave it (1 Nephi 16:28). And what must have been most "curious" to them was the fact that writing appeared on the Liahona "which was plain to be read, which did give [them] understanding concerning the ways of the Lord; and it was written and changed from time to time, according to the faith and diligence which [they] gave unto it" (1 Nephi 16:29).

Like the Liahona, the writings in the scriptures give us understanding about the ways of the Lord. The more we faithfully, diligently feast on the scriptures and obey them, the more we get out of them. The writings don't change over time, but we do. Our needs and circumstances change. We grow in maturity, in faith, in our spiritual understanding; and as we do, we discover things in the scriptures that we never noticed before, writings that are *new*—to us.

The teachings in the scriptures are not all to be grasped at once—and that, to me, is one of the most exciting things about them. There's a whole lifetime of discoveries there for you and me, depth enough to guide us through the deepest trials of our lives, power to keep us pressing forward toward our own promised land. "Wherefore, if ye shall press forward, feasting upon the word of Christ, and endure to the end, behold, thus saith the Father: Ye shall have eternal life" (2 Nephi 31:20). My hope and prayer is that you will enjoy this great feast throughout your life.

Mark Ellison *teaches seminary in Springville, Utah, and serves as a high councilor in a Brigham Young University student stake. He served a mission to the deaf and later taught American Sign Language at the Missionary Training Center and at Brigham Young University. Mark holds a bachelor's degree in English from Brigham Young University and is pursuing a master's degree in educational leadership. He and his wife, Lauren, have three children.*

12

Come to the House of the Lord

Brad Wilcox

"This *can't* be where Jesus was born!" I complained to my parents. I was in second grade when my family had the opportunity to visit Israel, and I didn't think the huge, ornate church we saw in Bethlehem looked anything like a stable. Later we also visited Solomon's stables; and while I was pleased to see they still looked like stables, the only other thing I recall is needing to go to the bathroom and not being able to find one.

Another vivid memory of that trip was visiting the Wailing Wall. "Why are they crying?" I asked my parents as we watched men and women approach the wall weeping and praying.

Dad explained, "This is a special place for them. People come from all across the world just to touch this wall because they believe it is a foundation wall of the temple that once stood here."

Mom added, "The same temple where Jesus visited and taught, but that temple is gone now."

Along with the temple of Old Jerusalem, Israel's ancient tabernacle is also gone; so are the temples built in America by the Nephites. In 1841 the Lord said: "For there is not a place found on the earth that [I] may come to and restore again that which was lost . . . even the fulness of the priesthood. . . . But I command you, all ye my saints, to build a house unto me" (D&C 124: 28, 31).

Indeed, foxes have always had holes and birds have always had nests, but the Lord of all had no place to call his house (see Matthew 8:20) until those early Saints built a temple, and Latter-day Saints have been building them ever since.

What is a temple? What happens inside, and why is it so important? How is a temple different from a chapel? Why can't everyone go in, and how is what happens there supposed to help us in our lives? I don't know all the answers, but I love the temple and want to help those who have such questions understand why the temple means so much to me.

THE TEMPLE IS A SANCTUARY

The temple is a safe refuge from the pressures, cares, and influences of the world. Maybe the best way to describe it is by saying that the temple is a little piece of heaven on earth.

When I went to Japan for the first time, the environment, the language, and the food all seemed so different and foreign to me. Everything was unfamiliar. Then I arrived at the military base where I was to stay with friends. I couldn't believe how comfortable I suddenly felt. Finding that base was like finding a little piece of my home right in the center of that foreign country. In a similar way, the temple is a celestial base in the middle of a telestial world. When we go inside the temple, we do not encounter things that are strange or new. The temple is comfortable. It's just like home—our eternal home.

President Howard W. Hunter said, "It is in the temple that things of the earth are joined with the things of heaven. . . . The temple is a place of beauty, it is a place of revelation, it is a place of peace" ("The Great Symbol of Our Membership," *Ensign*, October 1994, pp. 2, 5).

A mother told me of a meaningful temple experience. She said, "I think the most difficult time of my life was when our baby died. For several weeks afterward it was as if I were in a trance. I kept asking, 'Why did this happen?' None of our friends knew exactly what to say so, for the most part, they said nothing. I decided to go to the temple."

While this mother was waiting in the chapel of the temple, she opened the scriptures, and the pages fell open to the story of the apostles in their boat during a great storm. They cried, "Master, carest thou not that we perish?" The mother paused in her reading and thought, *I know how they must have felt.* She continued reading, "And he arose and rebuked the wind, and said unto the sea, Peace, be still" (Mark 4: 38-39). The mother said to me, "At that moment I felt such a wonderful peace swell within me. I knew my baby was all right, and I knew I'd be okay too."

President Ezra Taft Benson said, "When I have been weighed down by a problem or difficulty, I have gone to the House of the Lord with a prayer in my heart for answers. These answers have come in clear and unmistakable ways" ("What I Hope You Will Teach Your Children About the Temple," *Ensign*, August 1985, p. 8).

The Temple Is a School

President Boyd K. Packer has written, "The temple is a great school. It is a house of learning. In temples the atmosphere is maintained so that it is ideal for instruction on matters that are deeply spiritual. . . . What we gain *from* the temple will depend to a large degree on what we take *to* the temple in the way of humility and reverence and a desire to learn. If we are teachable we will be taught by the Spirit in the temple" (*The Holy Temple* [pamphlet, 1982], pp. 6-7; emphasis added).

One young woman told me that before she went to the temple for the first time, her mother helped her prepare by explaining that an ordinance is a symbolic representation of a spiritual reality. The girl's mom said, "When you're baptized you are immersed in water, but it isn't a physical washing, it's a spiritual cleansing." The young woman learned that the ordinances we receive in the temple are also symbolic of eternal realities that can be ours if we live worthily. President Ezra Taft Benson explained, "The instruction [in the temple] is given in symbolic language" (*The Teachings of Ezra Taft Benson* [Salt Lake City: Bookcraft, 1988], pp. 250-51), and Elder John A. Widtsoe extended this same point: "No man or woman can come out of the temple endowed as he should be, unless he has seen, beyond the symbol, the mighty realities for which the symbols stand" ("Temple Worship," address given in Salt Lake City, October 12, 1920; printed in *The Utah Genealogical and Historical Magazine*, April 1921, p. 62).

Christ has always been the master teacher. Sometimes he taught directly, as during the Sermon on the Mount, and sometimes he taught indirectly, as when he spoke in parables. Similarly, in the temple we receive both direct and indirect instruction. Some of the teachings of the temple, like the parables, are for those who have eyes to see and ears to hear. Truth is revealed or concealed depending upon our own readiness and willingness to learn.

One day when I was in school, our teacher taught us in an indirect way. She put some examples on the chalkboard and said, "Look at these and see if you can discover what I'm trying to teach you." At first the class didn't take her seriously. I thought she would soon give in and tell us what we needed to know. However, the teacher just waited and didn't say anything. Some of the students became restless.

The teacher said, "Look, I'm not going to spoonfeed you everything. You need to take responsibility for your own learning, so think about these examples and figure the point out yourselves." That's when the students in the class began the inquiry process. It wasn't quick or easy, but we finally presented our idea to the teacher and she said, "That's correct."

One exasperated student complained, "So why didn't you tell us that in the first place and save all this trouble?"

The wise teacher responded, "Sometimes the process we go through to come up with the right answer is just as important as having the right answer." No doubt the Lord wants us to come to certain understandings on our own in his house.

Since the Lord ultimately wants everyone to learn the lessons of the temple, why can't everyone go in? Some of my nonmember friends once asked why they couldn't take a tour of the temple. I told them politely that, while everyone is welcome in our chapels, only worthy members of the Church may enter the temple (D&C 97:15-16).

One of the group became upset and said, "A house of worship should be open to everyone."

I explained, "Throughout history, while many entered synagogues and other places of worship, temples have been set apart for special purposes—not open meeting places for the general public."

Another nonmember friend in the group added, "Don't you remember that even Christ cleansed the temple of those who should not have been there?"

Many who are not members of the Church wonder, as my friend did, why they cannot enter temples. I like the explanation one leader gave when his stake took the youth to the temple to do baptisms for the dead as part of a youth conference. A girl who was not a Church member but had come with her friends was frustrated when she found that she was not allowed to enter the temple. The girl said, "I'm not a bad person or anything. I just want to watch my friends. Why can't I go in?"

The leader handled the situation by saying, "You can—when you're ready." He explained: "The temple is like a university. Its doors are open to everyone willing to prepare by first going through elementary, junior high, and high school. There are certain tests that must be passed, not in an effort to keep people out, but rather in an effort to help them succeed when they go in."

The Temple Is a Place of Salvation

I recall when an angry young man once told me, "In the scriptures it says God is love, but I don't believe that anymore."

"What do you mean?" I asked.

He blurted out, "How can you claim God is loving when by requiring faith in Christ and baptism he has immediately condemned everyone who has never heard of Christ or had the opportunity to be baptized?"

Imagine my joy in being able to tell this young man that a loving God has provided a way by which all can receive baptism and other vital ordinances, even after they die. In the temple we perform ordinances for ourselves and also in behalf of those who have gone before us. Just as Christ atoned for us vicariously, we can do vicarious work for departed spirits who did not have an opportunity to personally receive the ordinances of salvation.

In the days of Noah, God did not send a flood without also providing an ark his children could enter if they chose. Temple ordinances are like an ark. They are the means of salvation for all who choose to accept them. Some may turn their backs on God, but he will never turn away from them.

We can feel especially close to our ancestors as we serve them in the temple. Patricia R. James, living in Milan, Italy, performed temple ordinances for her two great-grandmothers, whose names she had found earlier after receiving spiritual promptings about where to look for them. Sister James said, "I felt their spirits so close to me that I even sensed their individual personalities. Reflecting upon this glorious experience, I realized that my great-grandmothers now had the keys to participate fully in the plan of salvation. More than ever, I felt the partnership between us" (see LaRene Gaunt, "Finding Joy in Temple Service," *Ensign*, October 1994, p. 7).

THE TEMPLE IS A PLACE OF SEALING

On a long-ago family visit to the Salt Lake Temple, my dad pointed out the statue of Moroni atop the highest spire at the same time my mom was explaining, "This was where Mommy and Daddy were married."

My confused three-year-old brother blurted out, "Way up there?"

My parents assured him that it was *in* the temple—not on top—that they were sealed.

I once read a newspaper story in which the reporter asked kindergarten children to define some difficult words and then he shared their humorous responses. One of the words was *marriage*. The reporter obviously liked the definition one child offered: "That's when you get sealed." The reporter spent the rest of the article reflecting on what an insightful and wonderful definition of marriage that was—to be bonded, linked, sealed. Little did he know that he had probably just stumbled upon a young Latter-day Saint.

When my wife and I were first engaged, my work required that I be away for several months. It was difficult to be apart, but the thing that sustained us was the knowledge that we were going to be married in the temple and belong to each other for eternity. We loved the songs on the radio about how love should go on forever, because for us the concept meant much more than a sentimental lyric or a romantic notion. Indeed, we had "what all love songs reach for, but never can grasp." (Steven Kapp Perry, "Neither the Man without the Woman," *Come to the House of the Lord: A Musical Presentation on the Holy Temples* [SLC: Deseret Book, 1995], p. 56).

Later, when some friends who are not members of the Church were preparing for their wedding, they were bothered by the phrase "'til death" in their ceremony. Trying to grasp the teaching moment, I explained that when my wife and I married in the temple we were joined for time and all eternity. My friends were impressed and promptly rewrote their own ceremony to include the same words. I tried to explain that it wasn't enough to desire the blessing or simply say the words. Without the proper priesthood authority, found only in the temple, such a covenant is not binding. President Howard W. Hunter said, "Let us reaffirm more vigorously than we ever have in the past that it does matter where you marry and by what authority you are pronounced man and wife" ("Follow the Son of God," *Ensign*, November 1994, p. 88).

Soon after my friends Shawn and Cindy Hoopes were married in the temple they discovered they were unable to have children. They waited for years before they were finally able to adopt two beautiful little ones. I'll never forget the testimony Cindy bore in church after their family had been sealed in the temple. Tearfully she said, "I only wish you could know of our joy when our children, dressed in white, were brought into the sealing room. Shawn just beamed as he looked at them. Anyone who could have seen the look in his eyes at that moment would never dream of suggesting that because our children are adopted they are not truly our real children. While we may not be a family biologically, we are surely a family eternally."

President Gordon B. Hinckley has asked, "Was there ever a man who truly loved a woman, or a woman who truly loved a man, who did not pray that their relationship might continue beyond the grave? Has a child even been buried by parents who did not long for the assurance that their loved one would again be theirs in a world to come? No, reason demands that the family relationship shall continue after death. The human heart longs for it, and the God of heaven has revealed a way whereby it may be secured. (*Temples of the Church of Jesus Christ of Latter-day Saints* [Salt Lake City: Ensign, 1988], p. 4)

The temple is a sanctuary, a school, a place of salvation and sealing. The work done within temples is absolutely crucial to our happiness and progress here and in the hereafter. No wonder President Joseph Smith wrote in the last weeks of his life, "We need the temple more than anything else" (*History of the Church*, 6:230).

More recently, President Howard W. Hunter challenged all members of the Church to establish the temple of the Lord as the great symbol of our membership. President Hunter said, "Truly, the Lord desires that His people be a temple-motivated people. It would be the deepest desire of my heart to have every member of the Church be temple worthy. . . . Let us be a temple-attending and a temple-loving people" ("The Great Symbol of Our Membership," *Ensign*, October 1994, p. 5).

I attend the temple. I love the temple. Wherever I have been fortunate enough to travel, I have sought opportunities to visit the temples—even those only under construction. No matter where I have attended, I have felt a true unity of faith while worshiping with fellow Saints, even when we have not spoken the same language. I know firsthand of the personal blessings of temple worthiness and temple worship.

As a second-grade child in Israel, I was impressed with the sight of people gathering at the Wailing Wall. I remember the reverence and emotion with which they approached what they believe to be only a foundation wall of a temple. Think of how they would feel if they knew—as we do—that they don't have to settle for a foundation wall alone. There are temples on the earth once more—completed, dedicated, sacred places where God speaks to his servants and manifests himself to those who love him (see D&C 124: 40-41).

***Brad Wilcox** teaches at Brigham Young University. He served a mission to Chile and loves to travel and try new foods. He holds a Ph.D. from the University of Wyoming and once served as a national executive board member for the Boy Scouts of America. Brad and his wife, Debi, have four children and live in Provo, Utah, where Brad currently serves as the first counselor in the bishopric of their ward.*

13

Using the Book of Mormon as a Guide to Missionary Work

Todd B. Parker

President Ezra Taft Benson said, "The Book of Mormon was written for us today. God is the author of the book. It is a record of a fallen people, compiled by inspired men for our blessing today. Those people never had the book—it was meant for us. . . . Each of the major writers of the Book of Mormon testified that he wrote for future generations. . . . Moroni himself said . . . 'Behold, I speak unto you as if ye were present, and yet ye are not. But behold, Jesus Christ hath shown you unto me, and I know your doing' (Mormon 8:35). If they saw our day and chose those things which would be of greatest worth to us, is not that how we should study the Book of Mormon? We should constantly ask ourselves, 'Why did the Lord inspire Mormon (or Moroni or Alma) to include that in his record? What lesson can I learn from that to help me live in this day and age?' . . . From the Book of Mormon we learn how disciples of Christ live in times of war. . . . In the Book of Mormon we find lessons for dealing with persecution and apostasy. We learn much about how to do missionary work" *(A Witness and a Warning,* pp. 2, 19-21).

Since we sing, "We thank thee, O God, for a prophet to guide us in these latter days"—let us allow a prophet's counsel to guide us in doing missionary work, by looking closely at the Book of Mormon for principles that we can "liken unto us" (1 Nephi 19:23).

Preparation for Missionary Service

Some of the greatest missionaries who ever lived were the four sons of Mosiah and Alma the Younger. Even though the sons of Mosiah and Alma had some serious problems prior to their missions—"they were the vilest of sinners" (Mosiah 28:4)—they repented and prepared themselves for the work. Alma 17 outlines why they had "much success" (verse 4) among the Lamanites during their fourteen years of missionary service in the land of Nephi. Their preparation is listed by Mormon in three categories.

1. They had searched the scriptures diligently and were men of sound understanding, strong in the knowledge of the truth (verse 2).

2. They had fasted and prayed much so they were filled with the spirit of prophecy and revelation (verse 3).

3. They were patient in long-suffering and afflictions that they might show forth good examples. They were used as instruments in the Lord's hands (verse 11).

Let's examine each category a little more closely.

1. *Searching the scriptures diligently.* Searching the scriptures changes people's hearts. President Boyd K. Packer has said, "True doctrine, understood, changes attitudes and behavior. The study of the doctrines of the gospel will improve behavior more quickly than a study of behavior will improve behavior. . . . That is why we stress so forcefully the study of the doctrines of the gospel" *(Conference Report,* October 1986, p. 20).

President Benson based an entire talk on Alma's insight that the "preaching of the word had . . . a more powerful effect upon the minds of the people than anything else. . . ." (Alma 31:5). President Benson stated, "When individual members and families immerse themselves in the scriptures regularly and consistently, other areas of activity will automatically come. Testimonies will increase. Commitment will be strengthened. Families will be fortified. Personal revelation will flow" *(Ensign,* May 1986, p. 79).

One of the greatest blessings of studying the scriptures is becoming acquainted with the true author of the scriptures—the Savior himself. In a revelation given to Joseph Smith, the Savior said, "These words are not of men nor of man, but of me; wherefore, you shall testify they are of me and not of man; For it is my voice which speaketh them unto you; for they are given by my Spirit unto you, and by my power you can read them one to another; and save it were by my power you could not have them; Wherefore, you can testify that you have heard my voice, and know my words" (D&C 18:34-36). Each of us can testify that we have "heard [the Savior's] voice" through constant scripture study.

2. Prayer and scripture study bring the spirit of prophecy and revelation. Within the first twelve verses of the Book of Mormon, these first two principles of study and prayer are confirmed. The account reads that Lehi is "filled with the Spirit," which was accomplished through prayer (verse 6) and study of a book of scripture (verse 11-12). Scripture study and prayer can fill any person with the Spirit. A person need not be a prophet like Lehi for this to happen. Alma states that the four sons of Mosiah had obtained the spirit of "prophecy and revelation." Is the spirit of prophecy and revelation available to everyone? What exactly is it? The Apostle John informs us that the spirit of prophecy is the "testimony of Jesus" (Revelation 19:10). In a revelation to Joseph Smith we learn that the "spirit of revelation" is the Lord speaking to "your mind" (thoughts) and "your heart" (feelings) through the Holy Ghost (D&C 8:2).

The Lord added that it was this spirit by which Moses "brought the children of Israel through the Red Sea on dry ground" (D&C 8:3). We sometimes make the assumption that the Lord just revealed to Moses that he should open up the Red Sea to let Israel pass through. It is true that the Lord planted that revelation in Moses' heart. But what of his mind? Was there a need for Moses to study the scriptures so his mind would be prepared to receive the revelation? By what process did the idea occur to Moses' *mind* that he could open up a sea?

Moses was raised in Egypt by Pharaoh's daughter. He had access to the royal libraries of Egypt and the writing of Joseph, Israel's son.

Apparently, as a young boy he prepared himself for his role as a deliverer by reading the scriptural prophecies of Joseph who had been sold by his brothers and taken to Egypt. From the Joseph Smith Translation we learn that Joseph of Egypt had prophesied of Moses:

> And I will make him great in mine eyes, for he shall do my work; and he shall be great like unto him whom I have said I would raise up unto you, to deliver my people, O house of Israel, out of the land of Egypt; for a seer will I raise up to deliver my people out of the land of Egypt; and he shall be called Moses. And by this name he shall know that he is of thy house; for he shall be nursed by the king's daughter, and shall be called her son. . . . And the Lord sware unto Joseph that he would preserve his seed forever, saying, I will raise up Moses, and a rod shall be in his hand, and he shall gather together my people, and he shall lead them as a flock, and he shall smite the waters of the Red Sea with his rod. (JST Genesis 50:29, 34)

The Lord also had previously informed Moses that he would have power over the waters (Moses 1:25). So Moses didn't just stand at the edge of the Red Sea praying, "What shall I do?" It was through his previous study and prayer that his mind and heart had been prepared for that moment when he needed to receive the spirit of prophecy and revelation.

3. Patience and long-suffering show good examples and allow missionaries to be used as instruments by the Lord. Although we are often anxious to share the gospel with whomever we meet, we must realize that people are in varying stages of readiness to receive it. Some people have been previously prepared (as in the case of Lamoni's father—see Alma 20:26-27), some need to be prepared (like Lamoni), and some people may even have an antagonism or a hatred that needs to be overcome (such as the Lamanites).

When the four sons of Mosiah first announced that they wanted to preach to the Lamanites that they might "cure [the Lamanites] of their hatred toward the Nephites . . . that they might become friendly to one another...that there should be no more contentions in all the land" (Mosiah 28:2), the Nephites "laughed them to scorn" (Alma 26:23). The Nephites also suggested that it would be easier to kill the Lamanites than to teach them (Alma 26:25).

How was it possible for the sons of Mosiah to overcome the hatred that the Lamanites had for them? As Alma said, "They were patient in long-suffering and afflictions and showed forth good examples" (Alma 17:11), which allowed the Lord to use them as instruments in his hands. Ammon's experience in the land of Ishmael illustrates this principle. To understand how Ammon overcame the hatred the Lamanites had for the Nephites, let's review how that hatred began. About 500 years before Ammon's time, Lehi died (approximately 580 B.C.). At that time, the Lord told Nephi that his brothers desired to kill him, and he was warned to flee into the wilderness—which he did. He took the records, and those of his family who would go, and fled into the wilderness (2 Nephi 5:1-12). This point in history is the origin of the hatred the Lamanites had for the Nephites, which they taught to their children for hundreds of years thereafter. In Zeniff's record, contained in Mosiah 10, approximately 160 B.C., the development of this hatred is summarized.

> And again, they were wroth with him when they had arrived in the promised land, because they said that he had taken the ruling of the people out of their hands; and they sought to kill him. And again, they were wroth with him because he departed into the wilderness as the Lord had commanded him and took the records which were engraven on the plates of brass, for they said that he robbed them. And thus they have taught their children that they should hate them, and that they should murder them, and that they should rob and plunder them, and do all they could to destroy them; therefore they have an eternal hatred towards the children of Nephi. (Mosiah 10:15-17)

The Lamanites' hatred had three major parts:

1. Nephi had taken the ruling power out of the Lamanites' hands (verse 15).

2. Nephi had left them in the wilderness (verse 16).

3. Nephi had robbed them of their records (verse 16).

How was Ammon able to overcome this hatred to the extent that the Lamanites would listen to him? Did he approach the Lamanites and start preaching immediately to them? Did he call them to repentance? No, and neither should we in our dealings with our friends. Let's learn a principle from Ammon and his success.

After reaching the Land of Nephi, Ammon separated himself from his brothers (Alma 17:13) and went to the land of Ishmael (Alma 17:19). King Lamoni was the ruler over that land. The Lamanites took Ammon captive and brought him before the king. The king had the power to cast him into prison, execute him, throw him out of the land, or allow him to stay (Alma 17:20-22). When asked what his intentions were Ammon did *not* explain that he was there to preach the gospel and convert Lamanites (although this was his intent), but instead he was patient in long-suffering and showed forth a good example. He said, "I will be thy servant" (Alma 17:25). Ammon's volunteering to *serve* rather than *rule* helped overcome the Lamanite hatred of the Nephites, whom they felt had ruled over them unfairly in the past.

When asked how long he desired to stay, Ammon replied, "For a time, perhaps until the day I die" (Alma 17:23). This made a great impression upon the king since the king had been taught to hate the Nephites because they "separated themselves" from the Lamanites. None of us like people who separate themselves from us because they think they are superior to us. Ammon's volunteering to live with the Lamanites (overcoming one point of hatred) and volunteering to be their servant (overcoming another point of hatred) allowed him the opportunity to overcome the third point of hatred.

The third point of hatred was that the Nephites had robbed the Lamanites of their scriptures. After the king accepted Ammon's offer to be his servant, the king assigned Ammon to watch his flocks. A group of marauding Lamanites attacked Ammon. He defended the king's flocks from the Lamanites by cutting off their arms. He did not glory in his accomplishment, or become conceited because of this great feat. He did not seek the spotlight to gain recognition, but rather continued to serve humbly. The king was greatly impressed after this experience. Instead of waiting around for the king's praise, Ammon went out "and fed the king's horses." This example resulted in the king's desire to know more about Ammon and the reason that Ammon was able to do these marvelous things. This then opened the door for Ammon to begin teaching the king. Ammon's patience, long-suffering, and good example were now paying dividends in softened hearts.

This enabled Ammon to overcome that third point of the hatred—that the Nephites had robbed the Lamanites of their scriptures. So Ammon taught King Lamoni by "laying before him the records of the holy scriptures" (Alma 18:36). At this point it was not just the king who was listening, but the king's servants as well, as a result of Ammon's example. Patience, long-suffering, and example all had truly allowed Ammon to be an "instrument in the hands of the Lord to bring salvation to many souls."

PRINCIPLES OF TEACHING THE GOSPEL IN A MISSIONARY SETTING

The account of the four sons of Mosiah teaching the Lamanites in the land of Nephi is only an abridgment of a more detailed account contained on the large plates of Nephi. But in his abridgment Mormon has preserved for us two great examples of teaching the gospel to investigators. One is Ammon teaching Lamoni and the other is Aaron teaching Lamoni's father. The first account is in Alma 18. The second is in Alma 22. They both illustrate the same basic four principles in teaching the gospel, which are—

1. Teach with simplicity.
2. Teach with testimony.
3. Teach from the scriptures.
4. Challenge the investigator to pray.

1. Teach with simplicity. Ammon began his teaching of King Lamoni by asking what he believed. He asked, "Believest thou that there is a God?" (Alma 17:25). Lamoni replied, "I do not know what that meaneth" (Alma 18:24-25). Instead of complicating the situation with details that would be confusing to the king, Ammon found out what the king did believe and then added information in a simple way. "Believest thou there is a Great Spirit?" Ammon asked the king, to which the king replied, "Yea." Ammon said, "This is God." Ammon inquired further what the king knew about God and where he dwelled. The king said, "I do not know the heavens." Ammon, again keeping things simple, said, "The heavens is a place where God dwells with all his holy angels." We may learn a lesson from this. Too often in our excitement to tell people of all the restored truths we've learned over years of time, we try to explain everything we know all at once to an investigator. This is a mistake.

In the New Testament the Apostle Paul explains that a baby must be fed with "milk before meat" (1 Corinthians 3:2). Just as it is premature to give an infant meat before he has teeth or has matured sufficiently to chew, swallow, and digest meat, it is also unwise to give an investigator too much "heavy" doctrine at first. A foundation of basic truths in a simplified context is best. We note that Ammon didn't detail the nature of God that we understand from the Doctrine and Covenants 130:22-23. He also refrained from giving the detail of the three degrees of glory (see Section 76) or the doctrine of three heavens in the celestial kingdom (see D&C 131) in answering the king's question about heaven. When Ammon's brother Aaron later teaches King Lamoni's father, he also uses this same principle of simplicity (see Alma 22:7-11).

2. Teach with testimony. After simple truths are explained, it is important that they are validated by honest, sincere, spirit-filled testimony. Without the Spirit confirming what one says, the teachings of the gospel are of little value to an investigator. It is only through the Holy Ghost bearing testimony to the heart of the person that a real knowledge of the truthfulness of what one says can be realized. Some people mistakenly believe that a testimony given with the Spirit must be filled with emotion or sentimentality or be very dramatic. This is not the case. Consider what President Spencer W. Kimball said concerning testimony: "Do not exhort each other; that is not a testimony. Do not tell others how to live. Just tell how you feel inside. That is the testimony. The moment you begin preaching to others, your testimony ended. Just tell us how you feel, what your mind and heart and every fiber of your body tells you" *(Teachings of Spencer W. Kimball,* p. 138).

President Howard W. Hunter said, "I get concerned when it appears that strong emotion or free-flowing tears are equated with the presence of the Spirit. Certainly the Spirit of the Lord can bring strong emotional feeling, including tears, but that outward manifestation ought not be confused with the presence of the Spirit itself. I have watched a great many of my brethren over the years, and we have shared some rare and unspeakable spiritual experiences together. Those experiences have all been different, each special in its own way, and such sacred moments may or may not be accompanied by tears. Very often they are, but sometimes they are accompanied by total silence. Other times they are accompanied by joy. Always they are accompanied by a great manifestation of the truth, a revelation to the heart.

"If what you say is the truth, and you say it purely and with honest conviction, those [people] will feel the spirit of the truth being taught them and will recognize that inspiration and revelation has come into their hearts. That is how we build faith. That is how we strengthen testimonies—with the power of the word of God taught in purity and with conviction" ("Eternal Investments," Address given to CES Personnel, 10 February 1989, Salt Lake City, p. 3).

The Book of Mormon tells us that Alma was found bearing "pure testimony" to the people in Zarahemla. The Lord himself tells us to simply "declare the things which ye have heard, and verily believe, and know to be true" (D&C 80:4).

3. Teach from the scriptures. The Book of Mormon records that both Ammon and Aaron taught from the scriptures. Note which doctrines each teaching experience has in common.

Ammon and Lamoni

"Now when Ammon had said these words, he began at the *creation* of the world, and also the creation of Adam, and told him all the things concerning the *fall of man*, and rehearsed and laid *before him the records* and the holy scriptures of the people, which had been spoken by the prophets, even down to the time that their father, Lehi, left Jerusalem. But this is not all; for he expounded unto them the *plan of redemption*, which was prepared from the foundation of the world; and he also made known unto them concerning the coming of Christ, and all the works of the Lord did he make known unto them" (Alma 18:36, 39).

Aaron and Lamoni's Father

"And it came to pass that when Aaron saw that the king would believe his words, he began from the *creation of Adam*, reading the scriptures unto the king—how God created man after his own image, and that God gave him commandments, and that because of transgression, *man had fallen*. And Aaron did *expound unto him the scriptures* from the creation of Adam, laying the fall of man before him, and their carnal state and also the *plan of redemption*, which was prepared from the foundation of the world, through Christ, for all whosoever would believe on his name" (Alma 22:12-13).

Both missionaries taught the basic doctrines of the creation, the fall, and the atonement. Elder McConkie has labeled these three doctrines as the "three pillars of eternity" (*Ensign*, June 1982, p. 9). The temptation to discuss exciting, mysterious, controversial, or little-known doctrines must be avoided. We must realize the difference between letting an investigator know all we know and teaching them only what they need to know in the early stages of their learning.

4. Challenge them to pray. Neither King Lamoni nor his father would have been converted to the gospel if they would have refused to pray about the message that was presented to them. Aaron told Lamoni's father, "If thou desirest this thing, if thou wilt bow down before God, yea, if thou wilt repent of all thy sins, and will bow down before God, and call on his name in faith, believing that ye shall receive, then shalt thou receive the hope which thou desirest" (Alma 22:16).

The Lord taught his disciples in Jerusalem, "Ask, and it shall be given you; seek, and ye shall find; knock, and it shall be opened unto you: For every one that asketh receiveth; and he that seeketh findeth; and to him that knocketh it shall be opened" (Matthew 7:7-8). Jesus taught the same principles to his disciples here in America. "Behold, I say unto you that whoso believeth in Christ, doubting nothing, whatsoever he shall ask the Father in the name of Christ it shall be granted him; and this promise is unto all, even unto the ends of the earth" (Mormon 9:21).

As a result of Ammon and Aaron teaching King Lamoni and his father using these simple steps, "thousands were brought to the knowledge of the Lord . . . and as many of the Lamanites believed in their preaching . . . were converted unto the Lord [and] never did fall away" (Alma 23:5-6).

It is worth noting that these Lamanites were converted *unto the Lord* and not to the missionaries. Although converts often love their missionaries deeply, their feelings for the gospel must be focused upon the doctrines of the gospel and not upon the missionaries.

Mormon summarizes the experiences of the sons of Mosiah in words that could apply to all missionaries everywhere. Mormon quotes Ammon's words: "And we have entered into their houses and taught them, and we have taught them in their streets; yea, and we have taught them upon their hills; and we have also entered into their temples and their synagogues and taught them; and we have been cast out, and mocked, and spit upon, and smote upon our cheeks; and we have been stoned, and taken and bound with strong cords, and cast into prison; and through the power and wisdom of God we have been delivered again. And we have suffered all manner of afflictions, and all this, that perhaps we might be the means of saving some soul; and we supposed that our joy would be full if perhaps we could be the means of saving some" (Alma 26:29-30).

May we all follow President Benson's counsel and use the Book of Mormon as we should so perhaps we will one day be "instruments in the hands of the Lord" to save some soul. If we do, we will then experience joy with that soul in the kingdom of our Father, just as the Lord promises each of us (D&C 18:8-10).

Todd B. Parker *set a state record in the pole vault in high school. He holds a bachelor's degree from Weber State University and M.Ed. and Ed.D. degrees from Brigham Young University. He has taught seminary and institute and has participated in EFY every year since its beginning in 1976. He is currently an associate professor of religion at Brigham Young University. Todd and his wife, Debbie, have eight children.*

14

Whatever Happened to the Stripling Warriors?

Matthew Richardson

One Friday night, I went to a local video store to rent a video for my family. I had forgotten how crowded video stores are on weekends, and I ended up standing in an extraordinarily long line. As I waited for my turn at the cash register, I couldn't help noticing the young man standing in front of me, who had a very distinctive manner of dress and presentation. It wasn't his taste in clothing or style that made him stand out as much as the feeling, attitude, or air he conveyed. There was a rebellious, almost angry mood that hung over this young man like a black rain cloud. He held the videos he wanted to rent in his hands, and their titles told me they were not the types of videos you would watch with parents—or especially your bishop! He was talking loud enough so I couldn't help overhearing parts of the conversation he was having with his friend. His language was unedited, vulgar, and distasteful. If his speech had been added to the dialogue of a movie, it would receive a rating comparable to those on the videos he was about to rent.

I kept reminding myself not to be judgmental; perhaps he didn't know any better. But then I noticed something that immediately caught my attention and sent my mind racing. It was a ring. While he wore several rings on his fingers, one in particular stood out. It was instantly recognizable, and in a weird way it immediately linked me to this young man. One of his fingers sported a sterling silver CTR ring. "Maybe his ring isn't an *LDS* CTR ring, and maybe the 'CTR' stands for something other than *Choose the Right,"* I reasoned with myself. But then I looked again. Sure enough, it was an authentic CTR ring, complete with the shield where the letters "C-T-R" were emblazoned. I couldn't help thinking, "Does his ring serve the same purpose as the CTR ring that adorns my eight-year-old daughter's finger?" She wears her ring (in spite of the fact that it turns her finger green) as a *protection* (hence the shield) and as a constant reminder to "Choose the Right." I wondered if my daughter's symbol of protection and reminder to do right would one day be nothing more than a piece of jewelry as she, too, stood in a video line making improper choices.

As I reflect on that night at the video store and my concerns about my own children in the future, I can't help thinking of Helaman's 2,060 (yes, there were actually 2,060) stripling warriors. Some may wonder how the stripling warriors relate to video rentals. Perhaps it began while I was teaching the Book of Mormon a few years prior to this incident, and we had just finished talking about Helaman's young army of warriors. One of my students asked, "Whatever happened to the stripling warriors?" At first I thought, "What kind of question is that?" Then, as I contemplated an answer, I realized that the story of the stripling warriors is somewhat incomplete. The account never really says anything about what happens to them *after* the wars and victories. Did they go on missions, live faithfully, or march off into the sunset and "live happily ever after"?

Most scriptural stories unfold neatly. They have a beginning and an end, with a lesson sandwiched in between. While scriptural accounts are not detailed versions of the daily lives of people, they generally contain enough information to complete the picture. For example, Nephi is a young man when we first meet him. We observe his departing from Jerusalem, travel with him in the hot and dusty wilderness, and even sail with him and his family on a voyage to the promised land. We watch Nephi grow into manhood, marry, and have children. Finally, we are saddened to read of his death. The story of Nephi is complete from start to finish. The story of the stripling warriors, on the other hand, leaves us to fill in the ending. We know that they survive the wars, but then what?

As I think about the "then what," it is hard for me to imagine one of the stripling warriors saying, thinking, or doing something that would be in the least degree wrong or evil. It is almost unfathomable to think of seeing the stripling warriors returning from their military campaign in glory and honor, and then, five years later, finding them inactive in the Church or involved in immorality, cheating on tests, robbing banks, swearing, or any other iniquitous behavior. Why does it seem so strange to think the stripling warriors would do anything but that which is right?

Some people might say that the stripling warriors would remain faithful because of who they were. Their success would be attributed to no other reason than the fact that they were—the *stripling warriors!* After all, we are talking about a large number of young men (Alma 53:20; 56:46) who were *exceedingly* valiant (Alma 53:20), courageous (Alma 53:20; 56:45), active (Alma 53:20), sober (Alma 53:21), obedient (Alma 57:21), and trusting (Alma 57:27), who fought ferociously despite the odds (Alma 56:56), did not fear death (Alma 56:47), and were exceedingly faithful (Alma 57:26). As we describe these young men, it is obvious why Helaman said they were "worthy to be called [his] sons" (Alma 56:10). We then conclude that they would *always* choose the right—just like other righteous people in the scriptures!

As we read the scriptures, it is important to remember that the individuals in the scriptures were real people. They had feelings, hopes, desires, weaknesses, and strengths. Far too often, we see scriptural characters as one-dimensional and lacking the color and tone of reality. The beauty of the scriptures is the clear and resounding witness of what can (and does) happen in *real* life to *real* people. The scriptures provide stories about life—not fiction or fantasy. When we read about Nephi, for example, I hope that we find a story about a real man who actually lived on the earth. Granted, he lived long ago; but nonetheless, he was probably like you and me in many ways. He had a strong desire to do what was right. He also had some contentious brothers who struggled with just about everything. Unlike the image some people may have of "scriptural" families, you probably noticed that sometimes Nephi's family wasn't picture-perfect and had an occasional disruption. Does that sound like your family? Perhaps some of us are just like Nephi, trying to be the peace-makers, faithfully doing what we are supposed to do, trying our best. "Even though we are *kinda* like Nephi," we wonder, "can we really ever be *as* good as Nephi? After all," we might say, "he was practically perfect!" But like you, even Nephi wondered sometimes if he was good enough. He felt at times that he was nothing more than a "wretched man" who was "easily beset" with sin (2 Nephi 4:17-18). The stripling warriors, too, like Nephi and others in the scriptural stories, were real people. They had to make choices just like you and me. It wasn't any easier for them to choose the right than it is for you. They were real people, living real lives, and fighting real battles.

If you can keep in mind that the scriptures are loaded with real-life stories about real people, then the stories contained in the scriptures can help you, guide you, and even encourage you to continue in your chosen path. You may find personal similarities with some of those scriptural characters and identify with them. In a way, I feel that I know the stripling warriors. I have read what type of young men they were, and I have admired the way they chose to live their lives. Therefore, when I think, "Whatever happened to the stripling warriors?" I am confident that they did do the right thing, chose the right, and lived faithful, happy lives. I am not saying that they were perfect, but I am confident that they were trying to be perfect someday, and I believe that they were faithful to the end. My reasoning, however, is not based on *who* they were, but on *what* they were.

My confidence in the stripling warriors' future is based on something that runs deeper than their obvious qualities of courage, bravery, and obedience. I have known many young men and women who were courageous, trusting, and active at one time or another during their lives, only to abandon these ideals for something less somewhere along the way. While courage, soberness, obedience, and other exemplary traits of the stripling warriors were important parts of the story, there was something deeper that motivated these young men to be courageous, faithful, and loyal. They had something that was more than dedication, determination, and willpower. They combined two ingredients that made their lives special and embedded their story in our hearts. What was the stripling warriors' secret?

It is clear that the young warriors of Helaman had *desire.* Elder Jack H. Goaslind called this desire "Yagottawanna." This means "that you have to *want* to do something before you will do it" *(Conference Report,* April 1991, p. 61). Alma taught this same principle when he counseled that "if ye can no more than desire to believe, let this desire work in you" (Alma 32:27).

The second ingredient of these young men's success was also explained by Elder Goaslind. He said, "Youth with sincere desires take initiative. They do good things without waiting to be told. They 'do many things of their own free will, and bring to pass much righteousness' (D&C 58:27). They *act* rather than wait to be *acted upon.* They are in control of themselves" *(Conference Report,* April 1991, p. 62). Thus desire (faith) and reflective action combine to form a unique power.

There is no doubt in my mind that the stripling warriors had a desire to do what was right. They clearly demonstrated the *yagottawanna* attitude as they gathered *themselves* together to enter into a covenant to fight for liberty and in all cases defend the Nephite cause (Alma 53:16-18). In our day, too, this combination of desire and action creates a force more powerful than raw determination, courage, or willpower. It creates a "spiritual power." Such power, according to Ardeth Kapp, "comes when we strive to be totally obedient to all the laws of God and make Christ the center of our lives" *(My Neighbor, My Sister, My Friend* [Salt Lake City: Deseret Book, 1990], p.161).

Here is where my confidence in these young warriors rests. They were filled with "spiritual power." Their desire and faith in the principles taught by their mothers were strengthened by their actions as they "put their trust in God continually" (Alma 57:27). Remember, these were young men who were "true at all times in whatsoever thing they were entrusted" (Alma 53:20). It didn't really matter what they were commanded to do—they did it. These young men were so trustworthy that they would not compromise or give up. Their firm and undaunted stance was more important to them than life itself (Alma 56:47). I hope you can now see why I believe you would never find a stripling warrior wearing a CTR ring and choosing wrong.

The battles in which the stripling warriors fought so valiantly have long since ended, but similar battles continue to rage today as evil openly attacks that which is wholesome and good. To vanquish the foe, spiritual strength is still required to serve as a foundation for courage, faithfulness, and loyalty. As the modern-day wars with evil intensify, a call for the youth to take initiative has been extended. Like the stripling warriors, it is time to gather yourselves and make your decision. Perhaps this is what President Ezra Taft Benson meant when he encouraged you, the modern generation, to make a stand. He said, "Rise up, O youth of Zion! You hardly realize the great divine potential that lies within you" *(God, Family, Country: Our Three Great Loyalties* [Salt Lake City: Deseret Book Co., 1974], p. 189). Think of the strength that would come if our youth would gather themselves together as stripling warriors in the united cause of righteousness, the prophet serving as their leader.

I believe that many of our youth are gathering themselves together, and are committed to a righteous cause. There are those who not only want to do what is right, but they are demonstrating their spiritual power by making righteous choices. This causes me to reflect on another experience I had in a video store several years ago. While I was trying to decide which video to select, I overhead three young men talking. They, too, were trying to pick out a good video for the evening. "What about this one?" one would ask as he pulled a video case from the rack.

"No, I don't think so," one of the boys would say. As they continued to suggest videos, I noticed that a great majority of them were of questionable rating and content.

"How about this one? I hear it is really cool!"

"No," their friend responded, "I heard it's really not that great—kinda boring!"

As they continued to move down the video racks, picking out one video at a time, only to put it back in its spot, I began to notice that every time a video was rejected, it was done by the same young man. I was proud of him, for I thought I knew what was really going on in his mind. Finally, two frustrated young men, numbed from constant rejection, turned to their friend and asked: "What is it with you? Why won't you watch any of the videos we pick out?" I started to smile as I pretended to read a video cover and waited for what I thought was going to be the reply. *Okay, let 'em have it, you modern stripling warrior!* I thought to myself.

"Well," the young man said as he cleared his throat, "you know we're going to have dates with us tonight." *You're doing great,* I thought to myself. *Don't bend—keep it up!* The young man continued, "and you guys know that Lauren's coming . . . and I know that *she would never* watch anything of questionable rating or content. She would just leave."

His answer surprised me. I was wrong in my initial assumption that I was witnessing a stripling warrior in action. In reality, I witnessed a stripling warrior*ette* in action! All three young men agreed that it would be better to rent a video that would be more appropriate, and they started looking for new titles. Little did this young woman, whoever she was, realize what a powerful impact she made on a group of friends. I am confident that somewhere, long before her date was trying to choose a video for her to watch, she had made a stand for what she believed in. I was impressed that these young men knew that she would not bend or compromise her standards, even if pressured by a group. What a modern stripling warrior!

Others have responded to the call to rise up and take a stand. I knew a group of young warriors who responded to the call during an awkward situation in their high school. It seems that their school was divided by a number of gangs and groups of people who attacked anything that was good and wholesome. In response to the problem, their seminary teacher gave every seminary student a CTR ring and encouraged them to wear the rings as a reminder to not only choose the right but to stick together as a group.

As the LDS youth wore their rings, problems began to arise. At school, students would ridicule the LDS students for wearing their rings. Eventually, the taunts turned to threats. One evening, a message was left on the seminary's answering machine; someone was threatening to cut off the finger of any seminary student who wore a CTR ring to school. Naturally concerned for the safety of his students, the seminary teacher played the message for his class the next morning and asked the students for their input. As they listened to the threat of losing one of their fingers, one young man told his teacher that he needed more rings. Ten rings, to be exact—one for each finger!

I marvel at young (and old) warriors who believe in a cause and use spiritual power to forge ahead in righteous actions despite pressure, threats, fears, and tauntings. I hope that if you wear a CTR ring, it is more than a popular piece of jewelry. I hope it is a symbol, like the title of liberty was for the stripling warriors, that outwardly declares your inward desires and beliefs.

The gospel of Jesus Christ is calling for young (stripling) warriors. We need individuals who will gather together to claim the noble traits of the stripling warriors of old—warriors who will be "true at all times in whatsoever thing they were intrusted" (Alma 53:20). I believe that each of you is one of the warriors who can make a significant difference, if you will but choose to do so. God bless you in exercising "spiritual power." Rise up, O youth of Zion—*yagottawanna!*

Matthew Richardson *is an assistant professor at Brigham Young University in the Department of Church History and Doctrine. He served a mission to Denmark and holds a doctoral degree in Educational Leadership. Matt serves as a bishop and enjoys sports, traveling, and making Mickey Mouse pancakes on Saturday mornings. He and his wife, Lisa, have four children.*

15

THE THIRD MAGIC WORD

Vickey Pahnke

Remember when you were little and your parents taught you two "magic words"? Remember that whenever you used those magic words "please" and "thank you," there was a better chance you would get a positive response from Mom or Dad? I suppose what made the "magic" was that it magically transformed us into more polite, appreciative little people. I wonder what happens to some of us that, when we grow older, the "magic words" seem to lose their magic—at least to us. We may not use them as often. We might feel like, "What's the use?" As our self-doubts enter and grow, our thoughts may become negative or pitiful. Things don't seem very magical at all.

It seems to me that a way to regain that magic—those feelings of happiness and self-worth, and that ability to be more positive—is to go back to the "magic words" of our childhood. Many times it isn't as necessary to verbalize the feelings as it is just to *have* them.

There's a third "magic word" and it can make tremendous positive differences in our lives. This word is *gratitude*. Gratitude is a measure of appreciation in our souls for big things and little things and all kinds of in-between-things.

Have you ever arisen early enough to see the sun come up and watch the light filter through the heavens with glorious colors? Remember feeling the peace and the awe with the recognition that

Father provided such a beautiful thing for you to enjoy? Did you take a few minutes and thank him for that experience? I bet you did. And I bet he smiled down at you for remembering to express your thanks.

Gratitude is an amazing *trans-form-ative* force that can allow us to better enjoy our days and better choose our thoughts and activities. Instead of thinking about what's wrong with our lives, we focus on what is right. Instead of comparing ourselves to others and feeling cheated, we can appreciate another's blessings or abilities without losing sight of our own talents and gifts. There is an old poem that beautifully puts into perspective some initial thoughts on gratitude.

Today, upon a bus I saw a lovely girl with golden hair.
I envied her, she seemed so gay, and wished I were as fair
When suddenly she rose to leave, I saw her hobble down the aisle
She had one leg and wore a crutch, and as she passed—a smile.
O God, forgive me when I whine, I have two legs, the world is mine.

And then I stopped to buy some sweets. The lad who sold them had such charm,
I talked with him. He seemed so glad. If I were late 'twould do no harm.
As I left he said to me, "Thank you, you have been so kind.
It's nice to talk to folks like you. You see," he said, "I'm blind."
O God, forgive me when I whine. I have two eyes, the world is mine.

Later, walking down the street I saw a child with eyes of blue.
He stood and watched the others play. It seemed he knew not what to do.
I stopped a moment, then I said, "Why don't you join the others, dear?"
He looked ahead without a word and then I knew—he could not hear.
O God, forgive me when I whine. I have two ears, the world is mine.

With legs to take me where I'd go,
With eyes to see the sunsets' glow,
With ears to hear what I should know,
O God forgive me when I whine—
I'm blessed, indeed. The world is mine.

Author unknown

Once I asked a group of young men and young women about the things they were grateful for. It was an interesting few minutes. Some quickly popped their hands up, and when called upon, could rattle off lots of things for which they were thankful. Others said it would be a lot easier to share things that made them depressed or upset. The difference in answers showed in their attitudes. The difference in attitudes showed in their countenance. I could see that some of my young friends had temporarily lost the "magic."

Now, just for the record, there have been times when I've lost the magic, when it seemed pretty hard to count a whole lot of blessings, when I didn't *want to* think about things to be grateful for. I'd rather swim in my misery, thank you. But when the light dawned in my sad spirit, it was easy to see that Satan had temporarily shut my eyes to my blessings and stolen the light of truth regarding the importance of gratitude.

Maybe we could learn a few lessons in gratitude from those who have been such good examples of it. Imagine being one of Lehi's children. You are part of a prosperous family. You have riches, position, property . . . the works. One day your father calls a family council and says, "Guess what—we are going to leave behind our home and property, our riches and our position, and travel in the wilderness. We don't know exactly where we are going, or how long it will take us to get there, or what will happen along the way. Say goodbye to your friends, and we are out of here."

Now imagine how thrilled you would be at this point. What would your "gratitude quotient" be? Probably not very high.

You leave most everything behind, and even though you are confused and scared, you watch your father move forward with unwavering faith as you travel further from Jerusalem. Imagine the lesson you would learn from Father Lehi as he "built an altar of stones, and made an offering unto the Lord, and gave thanks unto the Lord" (1 Nephi 2:7). Now this was done after only the first few days in the wilderness. There were still many more days and nights, concerns and difficulties to contend with, but Lehi taught from the beginning that gratitude was a most important principle. I'm sure that their gratitude quotient made it a little better for this humble and mostly obedient family. The "magic words" did not make the troubles disappear, but the trials were easier to bear for those of Lehi's group who chose to show gratitude and obedience, and be Christlike as they journeyed to the Promised Land.

What is your wilderness? What is your tempest? What is your heartache? Is it possible to make an offering unto the Lord of some kind and give thanks for the many things that are right in our lives even in the midst of our difficulties? If our eyes will allow us to see, our view of the world and all that is in it will improve. Even when our heart is breaking, even when those around us may ridicule our faith or disregard our insight, we can stand and verbalize our gratitude for good things.

Remember Alma and Amulek? Wouldn't it be great if we could follow their examples? When Korihor confronted Alma, Alma responded, "The scriptures are laid before thee, yea, and all things denote there is a God; yea, even the earth, and all things that are upon the face of it, yea, and its motion, yea, and also all the planets which move in their regular form do witness that there is a Supreme Creator" (Alma 30:44). Alma was unfailingly grateful for all these things, and he could see their creator in them. And then there was his mission companion, Amulek, who taught that we should "live in thanksgiving daily, for the many mercies and blessings which [God] doth bestow upon [us]" (Alma 34:38).

Gratitude can hold us together even when we seem to be falling apart. Gratitude can warm us even when others are freezing us out. It can lift us up when the circumstances of life seem to drag us down. Gratitude is something each of us can develop, regardless of our situation.

I learned a little bit about the beauty of gratitude from a wonderful friend named Bart. I met Bart a few years ago while working with a friend on the theme song for the Special Olympics organization. Bart is a participant in the Special Olympics competition. He is mentally handicapped and physically challenged. He cannot walk straight and upright because his legs are severely bowed and bent. He cannot communicate clearly because of a speech impediment, and he has the mental age of a small child. I have never seen Bart when he wasn't smiling, however. He has been a constant example of courage, good cheer, and gratitude. When he was about thirty, he received his Eagle Scout award. I was there for the presentation and watched grown men weep because of their love for Bart. Those who worked with him described how full of good will and unfailing thankfulness Bart had always been. When the award was presented, I wept as Bart stood to give the victory sign, then embraced his mother and father, his countenance radiating absolute happiness. I will never forget him approaching my friend, placing his hands on my friend's shoulders, and saying, "Remember who you are—Heavenly Father loves you." Bart's speech was hard to understand, but the lesson taught and the Spirit that taught it, was clear.

Bart is a great example of one who is filled with the spirit of gratitude. His face glows with the magic some of us left behind when we moved out of our childhood.

I have heard it said that there are *miracles* and *coincidences.* A *miracle* is God's way of revealing his presence. A *coincidence* is God's way of remaining anonymous. How many times have we heard someone remark, "Wasn't that a coincidence?!", never understanding that a loving Father in Heaven has provided these blessings in our lives. As our gratitude quotient grows, so will our recognition of the blessings our Father so lovingly offers.

Sometimes, just looking for those gifts makes it easier to recognize them. And offering gifts that can be accepted with gratitude will ease our own burdens and strengthen our souls. Imagine that a pat on the back, a handshake, a hug, or a smile could be a magical miracle for someone you know. Imagine that paying an honest compliment could actually turn another's day (or life) around. Imagine that a good word offered to a stranger could be the "coincidence" needed to take off their blinders and allow their vision of themselves and their world to improve. Wow!! *You* can do that. You will find that your prayers will change. They will include gratitude for more of the personal blessings you have received and will include gratitude for the blessings of making a positive difference in another's life.

Regardless of the tumult in our lives, there are reasons to rejoice. No matter the destruction around us, there is reason to seek the magic of gratitude for good things. We can be as the people in 3 Nephi whose "mourning was turned into joy, and their lamentations into the praise and thanksgiving unto the Lord Jesus Christ, their Redeemer" (3 Nephi 10:10).

I have often felt uplifted by the kind words of someone who came up to me after a teaching experience. They may have never known how important their words of encouragement and love were to me, because my expression of thanks was inadequate. Maybe you have been one of those who have been such a blessing in my life. Thank you. Thank you for being willing to come outside your comfort zone and share feelings of gratitude. Thank you for following the Savior's admonition to love one another. Thank you for encouraging me by using the "magic words." I am sure you have done the same for many others.

Now, as you finish reading this article and think about the few examples I have shared, and think of some of your own, will you make a decision? Will you determine to go back to the magic of your childhood and make the "magic words" a bigger part of your life? Will you decide to whine less and appreciate more? Will you choose to embrace the gospel and its principles, and the brothers and sisters who travel in this wilderness with you?

If ever we see one another, offer me a handshake or a hug; let me know how you are doing with the "magic words." I'll do the same. Let's help each other. Let's pray for strength and determination and for more gratitude. Let's become part of the miracle. Let's be on the Lord's errand and be part of a "coincidence" that changes another's life for the better.

I will if you will. No . . . I will even if you aren't quite ready to. And I will pray for us all to better understand the magic of gratitude. I think of the hymn "More Holiness Give Me," and smile when I realize that gratitude is in itself a gift. It is a gift free for all who will take and use and enjoy it.

It is my hope and prayer that each one of us will clearly see how we are blessed in so many ways. As the poem I shared earlier says, the world is indeed ours. Gratitude will not make the road carefree but it will make the journey to our Promised Land a better, more magical one. That is a promise from a loving Heavenly Father and Elder Brother who want us to come happily, thankfully home.

Vickey Pahnke *attended Brigham Young University. She is currently completing her master's degree in communications. She works as a songwriter, vocalist, and producer. She loves mountains, music, cooking, teaching, traveling, and being a mom. Vickey and her husband, Bob, have four children.*

16

If the View is Good. . . It's Worth the Climb

Kim M. Peterson

Do you ever wonder why people climb mountains and hike trails? Or maybe you've hiked to certify at girls' camp, to get a merit badge, to get in shape, or just for fun. Whatever your reason, many of you know that the view can make the walk worth it. On the other hand, even if you earn a badge or certification, a poor view at the end of the hike can even make it seem a complete waste. For the right view, however, the longest journey and the hardest hike can be worth it.

People often ask why members of our church go on missions, sacrifice one-tenth of their income, read their scriptures, and obey the Word of Wisdom. All of these apparent sacrifices require effort. Like a hard hike or a long walk, obedience to these commandments can seem difficult. But remember, if the view is good, the climb is worth it.

My wife, Terri, loves to hike, walk, and climb. She finds great joy in identifying flowers, birds, and other wildlife. She would tell you that I hate hiking—unless there is the prospect of fishing at the end of the hike. . . I think she is right. So for most of our marriage, she has tried to get me to go on backpacking trips with her. Finally, last summer, after many reminders, I realized I was going to have to go on a backpacking trip with her to preserve harmony in our home.

Terri examined her maps, talked with some friends, and arranged for baby-sitting. Somewhat reluctantly, I packed my pack, loaded the car, and took my fishing pole. After a long drive, we found the trail-head. By the time we unloaded the car and started the hike, we only had about an hour of daylight left. Terri carried the map and we tried to figure out where to start. Near the trail-head there was a small river and a makeshift bridge. It seemed logical, so we crossed there.

Like my attitude about this backpacking trip, the attitude of some young people can have a big impact on their situation; a poor attitude can actually make one's membership in God's true church less than exciting. Some youth of the Church have seemed reluctant to be involved in the full activity of Church membership. Maybe you have felt hesitant to be friends with the other young people in your ward, to participate in family home evening, or to really learn something in seminary. Just as my wife and I made the decision to cross a bridge, some have made the decision to "cross over" to friends, school work, or possessions. After all, these things seem to promise happiness, and some people can't imagine that church, family, or scriptures can be enjoyable.

As my wife and I hiked, the minutes of daylight slipped quickly away. The trail seemed to disappear into bushes and was frequently little more than a patch of dirt between rocks and trees. It had rained steadily for the previous three days so every time our legs brushed against a bush or our feet walked through tufts of grass, water seeped through our clothes. As the light grew dimmer we finally agreed that we were lost. So, in desperation, we set up our tent.

You can usually tell when someone is lost. One of the strongest indicators that we are lost in this life is simply when we are unhappy. Alma taught us that "wickedness never was happiness" (Alma 41:10). Lehi taught his son Jacob, the purpose of this life is to have joy (2 Nephi 2:25). So many forms of unhappiness not only *result* from being lost but are actually *signs,* or indicators, that we are lost. The physical discomforts that result from drinking and smoking are indications that we must obey the Word of Wisdom in order to be happy. The remorse and guilt that come from immorality are profound testimonies of the happiness that can come from virtuous and moral decisions. The contention, loneliness, and feelings of being misunderstood that come from quarreling with parents are actually evidence of the potential love and harmony that could abide in your family. Compared with any of these negative feelings, my soaked pants and shoes were only minor discomforts, and could be resolved relatively easily.

Although we were cold that first night of the backpacking trip, we woke up well rested. With the dawn came a renewed strength and increased conviction to make it to the top. After a great breakfast of oatmeal, granola bars, and hot chocolate, we set out to find the trail. As we looked at the map in the daylight, we saw that the trail was on the *other* side of the river. We decided that the quickest way to find the trail was to travel in a straight line perpendicular to the direction we had traveled the night before. This meant we had to cross the river without a bridge; then, after several hundred yards, we found the trail. We also made an extraordinary discovery: when we found the path, there was no question that it was the path. The way was well marked and easy to follow.

Following the map might be comparable to keeping God's commandments and walking in "his ways" (Deuteronomy 26:17). A quick review of the word "way" in the Topical Guide (p. 567) reveals many comparisons to the path Terri and I found after being lost. Like recrossing the river, "the way of transgressors is hard" (Proverbs 13:15). Nephi's prophet brother Jacob illustrated the choice we can make between the "way of everlasting death or the way of eternal life" (2 Nephi 10:23).

There are many divergent paths that tempt travelers in this life. Many paths appear good, but only one path will lead us to happiness. Have you ever noticed that some of God's children always seem to know what to do in almost any circumstance? They rarely get angry or upset. They're usually at peace with their decisions and are generally examples of kindness. This is because they know they are on the right path, they know where they are, and they know where they are going. Just as finding and following the path brought relief to my wife and me, following the path of the Lord brings us gladness and renewed strength: "The fear of the Lord prolongeth days. . . .The hope of the righteous shall be gladness. . . .The way of the Lord is strength to the upright" (Proverbs 10:27-29).

Even when my wife and I found and followed the trail, the struggle and effort weren't over. The trail was long and at times grew steep; sometimes there were two trails from which to choose. Terri and I found that we had to use the map frequently to stay on the path. Fortunately, we never again had to wonder whether or not we were on the trail, and there was something comforting about knowing that we were on the right path. . . that every step we took was indeed progress. We hiked for more than three hours, and were never tempted to leave the trail again!

Just about the time I was beginning to feel that the trail was too long and steep, we mounted the crest of a bluff and an awesome panorama opened to our view. Vaulted snow-capped peaks surrounded a crystal-clear, glacier-fed lake. Meadows laced with delicate flowers and majestic pines lined the well-traveled path. It was spectacular, breathtaking, and well worth the hike! We quickly shed our packs and prepared our lunch. I even caught a fish.

Despite the hardships, I think I knew all along that I could make it. I even knew that the hike would be worth it. The interesting thing was how ready I was to give up. That hike was hard work! After carrying my forty-pound pack for three hours, sloshing in soaked boots, and having my hands swell from the altitude, even the austere beauty of clouds slipping off the skyline didn't make my feet ache any less.

Sometimes the effort to remain pure can seem tedious, tiresome, or even impossible. Heavenly Father doesn't excuse us from hardship. In fact, it is because he loves us that he allows us to endure trials, temptations, hardship, and challenges. In one of Joseph Smith's most trying moments, having endured the deplorable circumstances of Liberty Jail, and being separated from friends and family, he received the comforting instruction that all these things would give him experience and be for his good (see D&C 122:7).

Even though it was hard, my hike taught me some important lessons and it answered a question I'd always had. Have you ever tried to think about Christ for a prolonged period of time? Maybe you have struggled, as I have, to even concentrate for ten minutes or so during the passing of the sacrament. We promise at baptism and when we take the sacrament to "always remember" Christ. I wondered how I was supposed to "always remember" Christ if I could barely think about him for ten minutes?

My hike this summer helped me realize that there is a difference between *always remembering Christ* and *thinking about Christ.* As I followed the path, I learned that I could walk without thinking. I didn't have to think because the trail was clearly marked, and I felt safe on the trail. After a while, my steps became routine and my pace became rhythmic. I knew I was doing what I was supposed to be doing to get to where I wanted to go. Only when my routine was interrupted by an abrupt trip did I need to stop and intentionally think about where I was and where I wanted to go.

Just as I learned that I could progress along the path without deliberately thinking about each step I took, I've found that I don't need to be *thinking* about Christ to show by my actions that I *remember* him. For example, if I get in the habit of attending seminary every day, I don't have to wake up each morning and think about whether I'm going to go to seminary or not. I'll just get up and go automatically, because I've developed the habit. We can all develop the habits of a Christlike life by reading the scriptures, saying our prayers, and serving those around us. By doing these things, we can show Christ by our actions that we remember him.

We have all committed to make the effort to keep his commandments, take upon us his name, and to always remember him. To me taking upon myself the name of Christ at my baptism means that I will act like Christ in every situation. That means I will keep the commandments. And if I have mastered the habit of a Christlike life, this will show that I always remember him.

Once in a while, I may stumble, just as I stumbled on the path. When we trip over these stones in our path, it's helpful to stop and intentionally think about Christ. When our good habits are interrupted by bad thoughts, wrong choices, or temptations from people around us, we might sing a hymn, remember a scripture, or partake of the sacrament in an especially prayerful manner.

Another lesson I learned from my hike was the value of a good companion. She was great! Even though she was tired, she would encourage and help me. Sometimes we would joke about how hard the hike was or how heavy our packs felt. Heavenly Father has given us friends, missionary companions, parents, leaders, and eventually spouses to help us in our attempt to return to him.

Another companion I learned to appreciate was the pack I carried. Even though it was a weight I had to carry for six miles, I was glad to have it. I was grateful to have my sleeping bag and dry clothes. Each time we stopped, I was particularly grateful for the package of Red Vines licorice and my bottle of water. Just as my pack made my trip easier, the companionship of the Holy Ghost is a wonderful gift to help us on the way back to our Heavenly Father. In Doctrine and Covenants 20:77 the words of the sacramental prayer indicate that the reason we take the sacrament is so that we can *"always have his Spirit* to be with us" (emphasis added). The word "always" may only have six letters, but it can span our lifetimes.

One of the things that helped me the most on our hike was knowing that many people had already made it to the top. In fact, just before the hardest part of the climb, we met a couple who had spent the night at the summit. Their testimonies of the great view and the closeness of the goal were encouragement enough to keep us going.

Not only have prophets, ancient followers of Christ, and ancestors made it back to Heavenly Father, Jesus Christ himself has experienced the very challenges you and I are facing. In the letter from Liberty Jail, Joseph penned these words of the revelation: "The Son of Man hath descended below them all. Art thou greater than he? Therefore, hold on thy way . . ." (D&C 122:8-9). In other words, Christ has experienced your trials and your suffering. What do you think the Savior meant when he asked the prophet, "Art thou greater than he?" Perhaps he is suggesting that our complaints and desires to quit make it sound as though we think we don't need to try, or shouldn't have to work, or are somehow qualified to escape suffering.

I am so grateful for the realization that Jesus Christ has personally experienced the trials of this life. As I contemplated the choices some youth had made to leave the path they had covenanted to follow, I wrote the following poem. Even though I wrote it over ten years ago, the emotions are still strong. I can vividly remember the agony of watching some teenagers for whom I cared deeply choose to reject the commitments they had made to follow Christ back to Heavenly Father.

By the Path He Trod

Whether a canyon's sheer walls
 or the river's swift danger,
Perilous, life-threatening pitfalls
 subtly await the careless traveler.

Safely winding through obstacles e're present,
 steadfast, firm, and narrow,
The curved path, treacherous and bent,
 lends safety to those who follow.

Hence, naively the traveler wanders,
 exploring at safety's expense,
Dangerous, mysterious wonders
 away from the path's defense.

Naively, through life's temptations we dabble,
 ignoring the commandments of God;
Learning as we travel
 safe or sorry by the path we trod.

Once, through a garden alone and bereft,
 traveled Jesus, the Son of God.
By the side, his friends were left,
 bringing us to him by the path he trod.

Paul described the view we would have one day in the presence of God: "For now we see through glass, darkly; but then face to face: now I know in part; but then shall I know even as also I am known" (1 Corinthians 13:12). I know that this view is worth the climb. Every once in a while I think I catch a glimpse of an eternal view. I sense the joy of residing in the presence of God when I read the scriptures. I feel the peace of the Holy Ghost when I keep the commandments. I know that together we can return to Heavenly Father by staying on the path.

Kim M. Peterson *is a seminary coordinator and institute instructor in the Denver, Colorado, area. He loves to ski and has been employed as a ski instructor during the winter months. Kim also enjoys cooking a variety of Eastern dishes. He and his wife, Terri, have one son and one daughter.*

17

The Prevalent and Pernicious Poison of Pride

Allen W. Litchfield

Food poisoning is the worst. In my life I have had bronchitis, bursitis, and a broken bone, as well as miscellaneous bumps, burns, and bruises. But I have never thought I was dying until I was poisoned by our ward Relief Society president. After a banquet at the church, some ham had been left at a warm incubating temperature overnight. (She says she wasn't trying to kill the entire ward, but to this day we aren't sure.) The next morning she went around the ward, charitably and generously delivering the ham to various unsuspecting families. Two of my children and I made ham sandwiches at noon that day, and a few hours later were in the throes of pain and agony. Our bodies, recognizing that they had been poisoned, worked hard to get rid of the poison, but the process was excruciating.

I saw the horrific results of food poisoning again during the October general conference weekend in 1990 in Edmonton, Canada. Some young female students at the Institute of Religion where I taught thought it would be nice to prepare a big batch of chili for conference broadcast watchers. They made the chili on Saturday and served it the next day to sixty or seventy young people between Sunday conference sessions. Everyone liked the chili and the whole thing went well until the afternoon session of conference began.

People started leaving the chapel, the rest rooms started filling up, and soon people were crying and moaning and lying on the carpets all over the church, their bodies writhing in tortuous positions. It reminded me of that sweeping scene of the casualties of the Civil War in *Gone With the Wind.*

Soon ambulances began to arrive and people were ferried to the nearby hospital. IVs were started to hydrate the most seriously affected and many stayed overnight in the hospital, but thanks to good medical attention, no one died.

After hearing these two horror stories and perhaps thinking about your own experiences with food poisoning, you might be surprised by this next statement. Food poisoning has at least two good points, and neither of those is that it is a good way to lose five or ten pounds in a hurry. The first good point is that the victims usually know they have been poisoned. Food poisoning is not slow, subtle, and sneaky, but rather it is potent, plain, and prominent. Those afflicted are usually immediately and overwhelmingly aware that they are sick.

The second point is that food poisoning is so ghastly and gruesome, even when it is not life-threatening, that it is greatly feared. People are highly motivated to get treatment and relief. Some people are so afraid of this kind of poison that they refuse to eat at fast food restaurants, particularly those in chains where one of their restaurants in another city, even hundreds of miles away, has been found responsible for an outbreak of food poisoning. Other people remember so vividly the violent painful effects of a previous poisoning that they will never again eat the dish that made them sick earlier, whether it's ham, chili, tacos, or whatever.

A much more dangerous kind of poison is the kind that *gradually* kills someone without obvious symptoms. This insidious poison allows the unfortunate person to feel fine, and perhaps even for a time enjoy the noxious substance, which leads to continued exposure to the poison and the final lethal effect on the victim. For example, nicotine and alcohol are two poisons that work like that.

People who are not aware they have been poisoned and do not know they are dying, tend not to look in a frantic or focused way for antidotes to counteract the poison. Alma 47 tells how the wicked Amalickiah administered "poison by degrees to Lehonti," his rival for the leadership of the army. The scriptures do not show that Lehonti knew he was being poisoned; he may not have realized the source of the problem even when he was dying.

The Book of Mormon is filled with warnings about various kinds of "pleasant" and less perceptible poisons, especially spiritual poisons. Take a look at the description of the people of Nephi at the end of Alma 1. The time frame of these events is about 90 B.C. Notice that the people "were all equal"; they shared all they had with the less fortunate no matter who they were, "they did not wear costly apparel," they had continual peace, they were "exceedingly rich," and yet "they did not set their hearts upon riches." Alma even gives us a list of their many possessions and material blessings in verse 29, including food, clothing, and precious things. This sounds like a wonderful people to live among. Try to imagine living in a Zion ward or community like that today. Everyone would be dressed nicely but not competitively. No one would go to school, church, or a dance concerned that they weren't dressed well enough to be accepted and admired. Perhaps not everyone would have the same number of shoes, but I am convinced that during this period no one would have had twenty pairs of shoes while others had none.

Now turn three pages in your Book of Mormon to the second half of Alma 4. The time is now 83 B.C., or seven years later. What has happened to this happy, successful people? They have been poisoned, and most aren't even aware of it. The name of the poison is mentioned five times on page 216. Look for the name of the poison and mark it. The effects of the poison are also itemized: the wearing of "very costly apparel," wickedness, the setting of "hearts upon riches," scorning and persecuting of others, great contentions, envyings, strife, malice, wickedness, inequality, despising of others, turning of backs to the needy, and the failure of the church to progress. I am sure that you have discovered by now that the terrible poison that caused so much catastrophe is called "pride" in these scriptures. This is the deadly poison later spoken of by Mormon: "the pride of this nation, or the people of the Nephites, hath proven their destruction" (Moroni 8:27). Centuries later the Lord referred to those events and reminded us in the Doctrine and Covenants, "Beware of pride, lest ye become as the Nephites of old" (D&C 38:39). Repeatedly through the scriptures, pride is treated as a highly toxic and hazardous substance.

Despite its nasty effects, the poison of pride is difficult to detect in ourselves. In fact, have you noticed how much easier it is to recognize it in others than in ourselves? So how are we supposed to tell if we have been envenomed? You may have heard some of those "You might be a redneck if . . ." jokes the last few years. Some of these little quips are funny and perhaps harmless. But at worst, these "definitions" of rednecks can be mean-spirited jests directed at poor, less educated people from certain parts of America. When we repeat them, we might even be demonstrating a prideful attitude that suggests we are better than "those people." I don't want to do that in this article, but I would like to borrow that catchy phrase and present some suggestions under the heading: "You might be poisoned by pride if . . ."

- You think Cher Horowitz (the girl in *Clueless)* is a major Betty (attractive female), but she doesn't spend enough time and money on her wardrobe (see Mormon 8:36).
- In your prayers, you thank God that you are the most beautiful, benevolent, the best and the brightest, and express pity for everyone who isn't you (see Alma 31:17).
- You live in a great and spacious building and spend all your time mocking and pointing your fingers at people who are enjoying gospel living (see 1 Nephi 8:26-27, 11:36).
- You regularly seek medical treatment for stiff necks, high heads, and being puffed up (see 2 Nephi 28:12, 14).
- You have a full-length mirror in your locker at school and another one in your car. Or you have many pictures of yourself in your wallet, in your bedroom, and in your car (like Peter in the motion picture *While You Were Sleeping)* (see Alma 39:11).
- You have an "I" problem—that is, you start every sentence

with the pronoun "I": "I did this," "I said that," "I think this," "I want that," etc. You are not just the center of the universe (or egocentric); you feel you are the universe (see Mosiah 10).

- You boast of your wisdom, learning, strength, beauty, possessions, or anything else that you think makes you better than others (see Alma 31:27-28; 38:11).
- You do whatever your little heart desires with little or no regard for how it affects others and especially how it impacts your relationship with God (see Helaman 13:27).
- You aren't just interested in improving or doing your best. What you want is to "excel" or to do better than someone else. You always compare yourself with others (see D&C 58:41).

Most of us can read through lists like the one above and not see ourselves. We can smile and think of others to whom such descriptions might apply. But the point is that to some extent, most of us have already been poisoned. Benjamin Franklin said this: "There is, perhaps, no one of our natural passions so hard to subdue as Pride. Disguise it, struggle with it, beat it down, stifle it, mortify it as much as one pleases, it is still alive and will every now and then peep out and show itself."

President Ezra Taft Benson suggested that pride is so common that it might be considered the "universal sin." In fact, it might be safer to assume that since the poison is so prevalent, we probably have been touched somewhat by it, and our task is to try to find out how to treat it.

To return to the passages in the early chapters of Alma, take note that the list of possessions in Alma 4 verse 6 is nearly identical to the former list in Alma 1. The only addition is "very costly apparel." The wealth of the people had not changed in seven years, but *how they felt about their riches* had and that made all the difference. Now riches and prosperity do not inevitably produce pride. Alma 62:49 says about the people of that period: "Notwithstanding their riches, or their strength, or their prosperity, they were not lifted up in the pride of their eyes; neither were they slow to remember the Lord their God; but they did humble themselves exceedingly before him."

Therefore, we know that the poison is pride and not necessarily riches. Sometimes people take a snippet of 1 Timothy 6:10 out of context and claim that "money is the root of all evil." But a fuller examination of the previous verse shows that it is "they that *will* be rich" or those who want to be rich that "fall into temptation and a snare, and into many foolish and hurtful lusts, which drown men in destruction and perdition." The next more famous verse reads in its entirety: "For *the love* of money is the root of all evil, which while some *coveted* after, they have erred from the faith, and pierced themselves through with many sorrows."

This is an important distinction, because some people think that pride is a direct product of *having* some desirable material goods or characteristics. They think pride more or less automatically comes to those who have something nice: riches, beauty, talent, intelligence, athletic prowess, fame, success, etc. But while it is true that we all know someone who is blessed in one or more of those categories who is also prideful, we should not conclude that there is a necessary connection. Nor should we think that the poison of pride can *only* affect those who are gifted and privileged. In my own twenty plus years of teaching the youth of the Church in seminary and institute, and at Brigham Young University, I have taught high-profile athletes whose names are everywhere, beauty pageant winners whose faces are everywhere, brilliant geniuses whose accomplishments are everywhere, and children of very wealthy families whose possessions are everywhere. Interestingly some are poisoned by pride and others—who are completely happy and humble—are not. Of equal interest is the fact that many youth (and adults) who can't throw a ball, aren't photogenic, never get high grades, and have no money are absolutely dying of the poison.

President Ezra Taft Benson taught us much about the poison of pride, showing the contrast between the sin of pride and "a wholesome view of self-worth," self-esteem or self-respect *(Teachings of Ezra Taft Benson*, p. 485). We ought to realize that we are dearly loved children of heavenly parents and are therefore of great worth. We should feel good about who we are and take some joy in our gifts and accomplishments. But that is not that same thing as pride, which

President Benson declared is always treated as a sin in the scriptures. Elder Dallin Oaks added that it isn't just the *having* but the "comparing of riches, homes, cars, position, degrees, or other attainments, appearance, talent, wisdom, or any other natural or acquired attribute or possession" that causes serious spiritual problems (*Pure in Heart*, p. 95).

Elder Oaks goes on to define the real poison as "an attitude that commences with personal comparisons with others and leads to demeaning thoughts or oppressive actions directed at other sons and daughters of God." That is the poisonous prideful attitude that leads to the prideful action condemned by the prophet Jacob in the Book of Mormon: "And because some of you have obtained more abundantly than that of your brethren ye are lifted up in the pride of your hearts, and wear stiff necks and high heads because of the costliness of your apparel, and persecute your brethren because ye suppose that ye are better than they" (Jacob 2:13).

President Benson said that "one of Satan's great tools is pride: to cause a man or a woman to center so much attention on self that he or she becomes insensitive to his Creator or fellow beings. It is a cause for discontent, divorce, teenage rebellion, family indebtedness, and most other problems we face" (*Teachings of Ezra Taft Benson*, p. 435). He showed that while most people think pride is a sin of the rich, beautiful, and successful who look down on others, it is equally a problem for those looking up by "fault finding, gossiping . . . living beyond our means, envying, coveting, withholding gratitude . . . and being unforgiving and jealous."

We cannot just surrender to this poison, claiming that since almost everyone has it we ought not to worry. The Lord has repeatedly warned us of its deadly consequences on individuals and groups. But what are we to do? Josh Billings offered one remedy: "One of the best temporary cures for pride and affectation is sea-sickness; a man who wants to vomit never puts on airs" (*The Complete Works of Josh Billings* [Chicago: M.A. Donahue Press, 1876]). But that is a little impractical in the long run, and regular vomiting every time pride arises might lead to bulimia, so instead I recommend the following ten suggestions from the scriptures.

- Understand the Lord's greatness and our own "smallness" by comparison (see Helaman 12:7). On a clear, warm summer night go outside, lay down on the grass, look up at the skies, watch the stars come out, and meditate about your place in the cosmos.
- Be ready to give all the thanks to God. Remember that the Lord is the source of all our blessings (see Mosiah 25:24). A famous football player publically gives God the credit for whatever success he obtains, even though he himself does the running and catching, because he knows that in the end, everything good comes from God.
- Pray for humility (see Alma 13:28). This may act as a vaccination against pride.
- Serve others at every opportunity (see Mosiah 2:17). Rendering regular loving service buffers our souls from the worst effects of the poison of pride.
- Build up people around you (see Isaiah 35:3-4). Sincerely strive to make people around you look good to others and feel good about themselves.
- Focus on eternal goals (see Jacob 2:18). This is a great immunization against pride.
- Be obedient to God (see Mosiah 3:19). Practice by being obedient to your earthly parents—unless they are asking you to do things contrary to God's commands.
- Develop childlike, not childish, qualities such as submission, love, patience, willingness, and sincerity (see 3 Nephi 9:22).
- Forgive others quickly, even if they don't "deserve" it (see 3 Nephi 12:24).
- Search for the Lord's counsel in all the things you do (see Alma 37:37).

Although my own patriarchal blessing twice reminds me to "beware of pride," I have experienced the poison firsthand and still struggle with it from time to time. I bear witness that life without this poison is better. I pray that you chosen young people of the kingdom will not be poisoned by pride, and that if and when you are, you will be wise enough to administer the antidotes the Lord has prescribed in his holy scriptures.

Allen Litchfield *is an instructor of religion at Brigham Young University. A former bank administrator, he has served as a seminary teacher and principal and as an institute instructor and director. Brother Litchfield enjoys reading and such sports as horseback riding and white-water rafting and canoeing. He and his wife, Gladys, are the parents of six children.*

18

The Lord's Standard: The Morality Issue

Mark A. Bybee

I heard a joke once that serves as a great introduction to this subject. A father of six children had been out of work for six months. In desperation, he was reading through the want ads in the paper and came across an ad for someone to work at the zoo. The man called the zoo and asked if he could have the job, but was told that he would need to come in for an interview.

The next day he went to the interview, but before beginning, he was told by his potential employer that he would need to raise his hand to the square and promise that the proceedings of the interview would be kept confidential, whether he got the job or not. The man reluctantly took the oath, then asked what this job and oath were all about. The zoo owner asked the man what he thought the zoo's main attraction was. Without hesitation the man replied, "Everyone knows that. It's the big ape!"

"Well," said the zoo owner, "this is the part you cannot divulge, because we would lose our business. The big ape died, and we need to keep it a secret by putting the ape skin on someone who can imitate the ape—at least until the new ape arrives in three months."

"That's me!" said the man. "I can do that! I was a gymnast in high school and college." The zoo owner then challenged the man to audition by acting like an ape. The man assumed a crouched position and began running, jumping, and swinging around the room, imitating the actions and sounds of an ape. "Wow! You're really good!" said the owner, and immediately gave the man the job.

The next day the man, dressed as the ape, went into the cage and was an instant hit. Everyone heard how the ape was performing and came to the zoo to see him. The crowds got bigger and bigger as time went by, and the front page of the paper proclaimed, "The ape has gone ape!"

About two months before the new ape was to arrive, the man had about five hundred people in front of his cage, and he was waxing eloquent. He was flipping and jumping and swinging everywhere, when all of a sudden, at the top of a swing, his rope broke and threw him into the lion's cage. He rolled a few times, coming to rest against the bars, and turned to find himself across the cage from the king of beasts, who lay across the cage with his head down on one paw. He knew right away that he was in trouble, so he began screaming like an ape and running back and forth along the bars in hopes that someone would rescue him from this situation. No one moved. As he looked again, the lion began to move slowly and stalk him. The lion then growled, curled his upper lip over his teeth, and assumed a position to leap. Just at this moment, the man decided that his family was more important to him than his promise to the owner of the zoo. He looked up and started screaming, "Help! Help! I'm not really an ape, I'm a man. Get me out of here!" The lion looked at him and said in a loud whisper, "Hush up, you fool! You'll get us both fired!"

This is a silly story, but it has a great point. After a while, the ape-man didn't really know who he was or who those around him were. It's always been a reminder to me that if we truly know who we are, and who those around us are, we wouldn't struggle nearly as much with the morality issue.

When my oldest daughter was born, I held her in the hospital room and realized what a tremendous miracle and blessing she was. At the same time, I knew what an awesome responsibility we had as parents. As I held that little baby girl in my arms, I realized that my number one responsibility was to help her get back to her Father in

Heaven, and that the most important thing I could teach her was that she truly was and is a daughter of our Heavenly Father. Knowing who she is would save her from so many challenges and protect her from so many temptations. As I realized these facts, I brought her little face close to mine and whispered, "Micah, I love you. You are truly a choice daughter of Heavenly Father. Thank you for trusting us enough to come to our home." Micah has indicated to us that this knowledge has been a key factor in helping her to maintain a virtuous life.

As we examine the world and its philosophies concerning morality, it's no wonder that so many of the Lord's children get confused. Prominent doctors and psychiatrists, yielding to the influence of Satan, insist that "It's only natural," promote "safe sex," and use other immoral phrases that suggest lack of self-control and a total disregard for virtue. The world uses such statements as, "If it feels good, do it!" and "Do your own thing," while forgetting that we should be practicing self-control and doing the *Lord's* thing.

The Lord has been very clear in his counsel when it comes to morality. Among the many counseling scriptures, he has said in Jacob 2:28 that "I, the Lord God delight in the chastity of women." I am sure that he also delights in the chastity of men. Speaking to his son Corianton on the subject of immorality, the prophet Alma said, "Know ye not, my son, that these things are an abomination in the sight of the Lord; yea, most abominable above all sins save it be the shedding of innocent blood or denying the Holy Ghost?" (Alma 39:5). This scripture surely puts the Lord's feelings on immorality into perspective. And in Moroni 9:9, Mormon refers to chastity and virtue as "that which was most dear and precious above all things."

I recall a story I once heard concerning a seminary teacher in a small town who was teaching his ninth-grade class the prophets' counsel concerning waiting to date until reaching the age of sixteen. That evening, the teacher received a telephone call from an irate parent indicating that her daughter had been offended and "put on the spot" in front of her peers. This woman asked the teacher not to cover that subject again as long as her daughter was in the class. The girl's mother went on to explain that she and her husband had chosen to allow their daughter to date at the age of fourteen because she was "emotionally, physically, and spiritually advanced and ready to date." The teacher said that he would continue to teach the youth the correct principles from the prophets, but that he would try not to embarrass her daughter.

One year later, this teacher went to the hospital to see his former student right after she had given birth to a child. He said he wanted to confront her parents and say, "You felt that your daughter was physically, emotionally, and spiritually ready to date at the age of fourteen. Do you think she is now ready to be a parent at the age of fifteen?"

What right do we think we have to try outguessing the Lord and his prophets in this matter? Certainly great wisdom and knowledge have prompted such counsel, because the Lord knows that prior to the age of sixteen a young person generally lacks the understanding of how to "bridle one's passions."

The Lord has spoken through his modern prophets on the subject of immorality. President Spencer W. Kimball spoke frankly on the matter when he said, "Among the most common sexual sins our young people commit are necking and petting. Not only do these improper relations often lead to fornication, pregnancy, and abortions, but in and of themselves they are pernicious evils, and it is often difficult for youth to distinguish where one ends and another begins. They awaken lust and stir evil thoughts and sex desires. They are but parts of the whole family of related sins and indiscretions.

"Too often, young people dismiss their petting with a shrug of their shoulders as a little indiscretion, while admitting that fornication is a base transgression. Too many of them are shocked, or feign to be, when told that what they have done in the name of petting was in reality fornication. The dividing line is a thin, blurry one."

Concerning kissing, President Kimball said, "Kissing has been prostituted and has degenerated to develop and express lust instead of affection, honor, and admiration. To kiss in casual dating is asking for trouble. What do kisses mean when given out like pretzels and robbed of sacredness? What is miscalled the 'soul kiss' (or french kiss), is an abomination and stirs passions to the eventual loss of virtue. Even if timely courtship justifies the kiss it should be a clean, decent, sexless one like the kiss between mother and son, or father and daughter.

"If the 'soul kiss' (or french kiss) with its passion were eliminated from dating there would be an immediate upswing in chastity and honor, with fewer illegitimate babies, fewer unwed mothers, fewer forced marriages, fewer unhappy people.

"With the absence of the 'soul kiss' necking would be greatly reduced. The younger sister of petting, it should be totally eliminated. Both are abominations in their own right" (Edward L. Kimball, *Teachings of Spencer W. Kimball* [Salt Lake City: Bookcraft, 1992 (10th printing)], pp. 280-290).

I often remember how young Joseph handled the temptations of immorality in Potiphar's house. I'm sure the temptations came often as Potiphar's wife pursued Joseph. He said to her, "How then can I do this great wickedness, and sin against God?" (Gen. 39:9). She didn't appreciate this rejection and grabbed Joseph's cloak, demanding that he be immoral with her. Joseph was so intent on keeping his virtue and being true to his God that he ran out, leaving his clothing in her hand. This was probably not the "in thing" to do, nor was it cool, but it was the *right* thing to do. That act got Joseph thrown into prison for thirteen years, but it also allowed him the right to receive the inspiration that later led to his becoming a great prophet, as well as the second most powerful man in all of Egypt and the savior of his Israelite family.

In October 1972 General Conference, Elder Hartman Rector, Jr. gave specific counsel on how to prevent situations leading to immorality. He said:

1. Never go into a house alone with one of the opposite sex.
2. Never, never enter a bedroom alone with one of the opposite sex.
3. Do not neck or pet.
4. Never park on a lonely road with just the two of you alone.
5. Do not read pornographic literature.
6. Do not attend R-or-X rated movies, and avoid drive-in movies.
7. Do not spend time in drinking or gambling establishments. (*Ensign,* January 1973, p. 131.)

In 1964 October General Conference, Elder Ezra Taft Benson discussed additional precautions. He counseled:

1. Avoid late hours and weariness.
2. Keep your dress modest.
3. Have good associates.
4. Avoid necking and petting like a plague.
5. Have a good physical outlet.
6. Think clean thoughts.
7. Pray. (*Conference Report*, October 1964, pp. 59-60.)

From the time I was very young, my father would remind me that God was always watching me, even if I couldn't see him. I heard this so often that it didn't surprise me to hear it again as I left for Ricks College. He said, "Son, I just want to say something before you leave." To this I quickly replied, "I know, Dad—God is always watching." He paused for a moment and said, "When you find yourself alone with a girl in the car, remember the others who are watching: Jesus, the Holy Ghost, and all of your dead relatives who have been invited to view." Even though Dad and I both knew that there was no doctrine supporting such a scenario, he will never know the grief and heartache he saved me from as, so many times, I looked around to see if I could see or feel Grandma's eyes on me. Isn't it interesting what we would do in front of God that we would never do in front of Grandma.

Reflecting on something my dad told me concerning God's watching us, I tried an experiment with my six-year-old daughter. I took her into a grocery store, put her in front of the candy counter, and told her to wait until I returned with the milk. Then I walked to the end of the aisle, turned the corner, and ran down the next aisle so I could see Micah through the bread rack. She didn't know I was watching her. Micah would walk up and down in front of the candy bins, take candy out of a bin, smell it, and then put it back. She loved chocolate so much that I knew it would be a test to see if she would take the candy. I never got nervous until Micah looked up into the mirrors at the end of the aisle and then walked to the end to see if she was being watched. When she walked back to the bins and reached for a bag of candy, my heart jumped into my throat as I realized she was thinking about stealing it. I wanted to play the part of the Holy Ghost and whisper through the bread rack, "Micah, don't steal the candy," but I realized that if I did, I would never discover if I had taught her right. At one point, I even started to cry because I wanted so badly for her to choose the right. She looked at the candy, smelled it, then finally threw it back in the bin and folded her arms tightly, shaking her head vigorously from side to side. I was so excited! I wanted to do a Toyota jump and scream "Yes!" As I walked out to the car, it hit me like a ton of bricks that God gets so excited when we make right decisions, and hurts so terribly when we make wrong decisions, because he truly is our Father in Heaven. I also realized that because he is our Father and loves us without condition, he has provided a way for us to have forgiveness through the atonement of his son Jesus Christ when we slip or make wrong choices. Isaiah 1:18 and D&C 58:42-43 both indicate that we can have complete forgiveness for sins that we repent of and give away to Christ. The time for virtuous and moral living is *now.*

I often wondered what the scriptures meant when they said, "And they twain shall be one flesh" (Matthew 19:5). My father said that the creation of a physical body for one of God's spirit children was the only creative power that God had given to man on this earth. He said that we should never, never tamper with that sacred creative power. All of these things made sense when Micah was born. I looked down at that little body and said, "Oh! I get it! The two shall be one flesh." I held her in front of her mother and said, "Look, honey, it's *us!*"

I challenge each of you to be virtuous and clean before the Lord and to never, never, never tamper with the creative powers that he has entrusted to you. One day, you will use these powers to create bodies for his children, and I bear testimony that your lives will be blessed for it.

***Mark A. Bybee**, an international business consultant in Roy, Utah, holds a master's degree in recreational management. He enjoys racquetball, the martial arts, outdoor recreation generally, and high-risk sports such as kayaking and white-water rafting. He encourages young people to "look forward," and to "look to the Savior for help." Mark and his wife, Lisa, have nine children.*

19

On My Honor

Gary R. Nelson

Several years ago an adult scouter named Dimitrious recounted a personal experience he had as a young boy growing up in a small village in Greece during World War II. In his village, several men had devoted themselves to acts of sabotage and hostility against the German Nazis to show their disapproval and resentment towards the war. Dimitrious explained:

> One night after the men had destroyed a hydroelectric dam, the villagers celebrated the achievement and then retired to their homes. Very early in the morning, I heard the sound of soldiers' boots, the rap at the door, and the command for every boy and man to assemble at once in the village square. I had time only to slip into my trousers, buckle my belt, and join the others. There, under the glaring lights of a dozen trucks, and before the muzzles of a hundred guns, we stood. The Nazis vented their wrath, told of the destruction of the dam, and announced a drastic penalty: every fifth man or boy was to be summarily shot. A sergeant made the fateful count, and the first group was designated and executed. Then came the row in which I was standing. To my horror, I could see that I would be the final person designated for execution. The

> soldier stood before me, the angry headlights dimming my vision. He gazed intently at the buckle of my belt. It carried on it the Scout insignia. I had earned the belt buckle as a Boy Scout for knowing the Oath and the Law of Scouting. The tall soldier pointed at the belt buckle, then raised his right hand in the Scout sign. I shall never forget the words he spoke to me: "Run, boy, run!" I ran. I lived. Today I serve Scouting, that boys may still dream dreams and live to fulfill them. (Told by Thomas S. Monson, "Run, Boy, Run," *Ensign*, November, 1982, p. 19)

The scout oath Dimitrious learned to earn the belt buckle that saved his life states in part: "ON MY HONOR I will do my best to do my duty. . . ." *(Boy Scout Handbook*, Irving, Texas: Boy Scouts of America, 1990, p. 549-551). In a similar fashion, the Young Women's program emphasizes, in its Young Women's Values, the value of INTEGRITY. How greatly today do our youth in the Church stand in need of these ideals of *honor* and *integrity.*

While teaching seminary in Roy, Utah, I challenged my ninth-grade students to read and re-read the Book of Mormon. To acknowledge their efforts, I placed a little card stock facsimile of the gold plates on the classroom wall with the student's name. I would attach a gold star for each time they read the Book of Mormon. Five years later I received an interesting letter in a temple wedding announcement from a young woman whom I had taught in ninth grade. She asked forgiveness from me. The six gold stars that had been placed on the paper book had not been honestly earned. In fact, she admitted, "I never read the Book of Mormon one time that year."

My next seminary assignment was at Dixie High Seminary in St. George, Utah. During the spring of 1996, a group of twelve seniors from St. George attended the Dixie High School state play-off games in Orem and stayed at a motel in Springville. One evening, after the tournament games concluded, they decided to watch an explicit, pornographic movie on a pay-per-view box in one of the rooms. One of the young men present attended my seminary class that year, and he determined that he would not be involved in such filth. Feeling strongly that it would be offensive to his spirit and standards, he stood up and told the group that he would not participate in this activity and walked out. The only place he could find to sleep was in the back of a friend's truck. Since the doors were locked, he made himself as comfortable as possible in the back of the truck on that cold March night. Four other boys followed his example and went back to their rooms. At the expense of momentary pleasure and the loss of peer approval, this young man stood up for principles of honesty and integrity.

"Don't rationalize that wrong is right," reads the statement from the First Presidency in the "For the Strength of Youth" pamphlet. "Being honest includes having the courage to do what you know to be right." This young man had the courage to do what he knew was right. Today he continues to stand for truth as he serves a full-time mission in South America.

The "For the Strength of Youth" pamphlet continues: "Be honest with yourself and others, including the Lord. Honesty with yourself brings peace and self-respect. When you are honest with others, you build a foundation for friendship and trust. For example, honesty with your parents can help to establish a trusting and lasting relationship with them. Dishonesty hurts you and usually hurts other people as well. Being honest with the Lord will bring his trust and blessings. Lying damages your spirit. Stealing or shoplifting does the same thing, as does cheating in school. The Lord said: 'Thou shalt not steal. Thou shalt not bear false witness' (Exodus 20:15-16)" (1990, pp. 9-10.).

Recently, I conducted a survey of youth, ages 14-18, regarding honesty. It consisted of 700 young people from the ninth through twelfth grades. I entitled the survey "Honestly Speaking." Following is a breakdown of some of the questions and their results:

	Always	Almost Always	Sometimes	Seldom	Never
1. I classify myself as a basically honest person.	16%	65%	13%	6%	0%
2. If I can, I will cheat on a test or assignment to improve my score or grade.	2%	6%	22%	34%	36%

	Always	Almost Always	Some-times	Seldom	Never
3. If I were to back into a parked car in a parking lot and cause a dent in the car and knew no one saw it, I would still notify the owner.	49%	23%	12%	8%	8%
4. If someone gave me too much change, I would return it to the clerk.	46%	26%	13%	9%	6%
5. I would make up an excuse to break a date with a person so I could go out with someone I like better.	3%	5%	22%	28%	42%
6. I would lie about my age in order to get into a dance with those 18 and older.	5%	4%	12%	12%	67%
7. If I found $20 on the floor in a store, I would turn it in to the manager to see if anyone claimed it.	35%	17%	17%	15%	16%
8. I would lie to my parents, school administrator or police officer rather than get my friends in trouble.	6%	10%	24%	30%	30%

	Strongly Agree	Agree	Disagree	Seldom	Never
9. I have a large packet due in history. I don't have time to do it, but need a good score. I'll borrow someone else's answers because *borrowing* answers is not cheating.	5%	20%	34%	19%	22%

It appears from the quantitative data received from the survey that we have a spectrum of differences in opinion on what is honest or dishonest.

It has been said, "It is time to teach honor to America. It is time to acknowledge that an honest man is the noblest work of God. It is time to remember that when the grown-up sheep wander away from the fold, they usually lead the lambs astray." The thirteenth Article of Faith says, "We believe in being honest. . . ."

Several years ago in general conference, President Hinckley, then one of the Twelve Apostles, gave the following insights on honesty:

> Among many unsigned letters I have received was one of particular interest. It contained a $20 bill and a brief note which stated that the writer had come to my home many years ago. When there was no response to the bell, he had tried the door and, finding it unlocked, had entered and walked about. On the dresser he saw a $20 bill, took it, and left. Through the years his conscience had bothered him and he was now returning the money. . . .
>
> Our papers carried a similar story the other day [continued President Hinckley]. The state of Utah received an unsigned note together with $200. The note read: "The enclosed is for materials used over the years I worked for the state—such as envelopes, paper, stamps, etc." . . .
>
> Fortunately there are still those who observe such principles of personal rectitude. Recently we rode a train from Osaka to Nagoya, Japan. At the station were friends to greet us, and in the excitement my wife left her purse on the train. We called the Tokyo station to report it. When the train arrived at its destination some three hours later, the railroad telephoned to say the purse was there. We were not returning via Tokyo, and more than a month passed before it was delivered to us in Salt Lake City. Everything left in the purse was there when it was returned. ("An Honest Man—God's Noblest Work," *Ensign*, November, 1976, p. 60)

Like the Hinckleys, I traveled from Osaka to Nagoya, Japan, and observed the honesty of the Japanese people. I saw no guards or security. My wife and I were also fortunate to have many Japanese students live with our family. One particular girl named Fumi Sato lived with us for three years. Her parents lived in Tokyo, and she came to the United States to learn English and graduate from college. She graduated from Dixie Junior College and then went on to graduate from the University of Nevada in Las Vegas. While attending Dixie College, she left her textbooks and tennis racket in her class while she bought a sandwich to eat at the cafeteria. When she returned, her tennis racquet was gone. She asked others, but nobody had seen it. She had never had anything stolen before, and she could not believe that anyone would actually steal. In her country, nobody would steal a tennis racquet, or anything else for that matter, because of the high standards of integrity the people place on themselves. Replacing the racquet was not a problem, as her father owns a retail sporting goods store in Tokyo. What was hard to replace was the loss of trust and honor in the American people, which was dictated by the actions of one thoughtless person.

Do you have the Gehazi disease? The scriptures record this interesting account of dishonesty. In 2 Kings, chapter five, we read about the story of the Prophet Elisha and Naaman, captain of the Syrian king's army. He had leprosy and had come to meet the prophet to be healed of the disease. He, at first, rejected Elisha's command to dip himself seven times in the Jordan River, but later followed the sacred instructions and was healed. Naaman desired to pay Elisha for the miracle, but upon Elisha's refusal, departed back to Syria. Elisha's servant, Gehazi, seeing an opportunity to satisfy his greed, caught up to the caravan. He said Elisha had sent him for the payment of the miracle. Naaman gave him two talents of silver and two changes of clothing. He secretly took them to his tent, trying to hide his dishonest deed.

But when he stood before Elisha, Elisha said, "Whence comest thou, Gehazi?" Gehazi responded that he had not gone anywhere. Elisha then prophetically told him everything he had done to secure the silver and clothing, and then he prophesied: "The leprosy therefore of Naaman shall cleave unto thee, and unto thy seed forever. And he went out from his presence a leper. . . ." (2 Kings 5:25-27).

So, once again, now that you are familiar with the story, let me ask the same question. Do you have Gehazi's disease? Do you have problems with acts of stealing, cheating, lying, or immorality that need to be addressed and repented of in your life? Remember Gehazi. You might not receive leprosy, but you may experience the pains and stains of sin. We must follow the counsel of Paul to "let a man examine himself" (1 Corinthians 11:28). It might be well to remind us of the words of Benjamin Franklin: "A small leak will sink a great ship." President Hinckley said, "'Thou shalt not bear false witness.' . . . Television recently carried the story of a woman imprisoned for twenty-seven years, having been convicted on the testimony of witnesses who have now come forth to confess they had lied. I know that this is an extreme case, but are you not acquainted with instances of reputations damaged, of hearts broken, of careers destroyed by the lying tongues of those who have borne false witness?" ("An Honest Man—God's Noblest Work," *Ensign*, November, 1976, p. 61).

President Thomas S. Monson has said, "A Latter-day Saint young man lives as he teaches and as he believes. He is honest with others. He is honest with himself. He is honest with God. He is honest by habit and as a matter of course. When a difficult decision must be made, he never asks himself, 'What will others think?' but rather, 'What will I think of myself?'" ("That We May Touch Heaven," *Ensign*, November, 1990, p. 46).

President Monson went on to tell of an experience of a young man in one of his classes who had succumbed to the temptation of cheating. He wore on his bare feet only sandals. With his books placed on the floor, he turned the pages with his toes that had been prepared with glycerine. President Monson said, "He received one of the highest grades in that course on business law. But the day of reckoning came. Later as he prepared to take his comprehensive examination, for the first time the dean of his particular discipline said, 'This year I shall depart from tradition and shall conduct an oral, rather than a written test.' Our favorite, trained-toe expert found that he had his foot in his mouth on that occasion and failed the examination."

Do you remember the example of honesty that President Monson highlighted in October general conference 1995? It was about the woman who had stayed in the Hotel Utah thirteen years earlier and had kept the room key as a souvenir. She enclosed the key with her letter of apology and asked for his forgiveness. President Monson records the following from his letter to her: ". . . though the key itself weighed very little, apparently this has been a heavy burden for you to carry for such a long time. Though the key was of very little worth, its return is of far greater value. . . . Please accept the enclosed gift with my warmest wishes" *(Conference Report,* April 2, 1995, p. 78).

The key had been mounted on a plaque and returned to the woman.

Doug and Geri Brinley of Provo, Utah, tell how, while waiting for a tour through the famous Hearst Castle in 1962, they happened upon Elder and Sister Howard W. Hunter. The Hunters invited the newly married Brinleys to take a drive with them as they awaited the next tour. They stopped at a small rustic store nearby. Elder Hunter found some licorice and counted out ten pennies to the store clerk. Later as the licorice was passed around in the car, Elder Hunter noticed that he had eleven pieces of licorice instead of the ten for which he had paid. Brother Doug Brinley says, "He could have easily overlooked the small error—after all, it was just a penny, and we were in a bit of a hurry to make the tour. Who would know the difference or care? I don't think he thought twice about it. He wheeled the car around and headed back to the store. He and I hustled in. To a different attendant, he explained the problem, apologized for the error, and paid the extra penny to the surprised clerk.

"We arrived on time for the tour, but I feel certain that Elder Hunter would have made the effort to pay the penny even if doing so would have made us miss the tour. What a memorable lesson in integrity Elder Hunter taught us that day. We have not forgotten that sermon from more than thirty years ago, and we remembered it every time we raised our hands to sustain him as our Prophet, Seer, and Revelator." ("Loved by All," *Ensign,* April, 1995, p. 19-20)

Several years ago a successful businessman I know shared with me the following story. He said one of his former employees showed up at his doorstep in tears and gave him an envelope containing $300. It was to pay back money that had been taken out of a retail cash register to support the woman's son on his mission. The restitution was made, the repentance complete.

At one point in early Church history, the Prophet Joseph Smith and Orrin Porter Rockwell, a personal friend and bodyguard, were falsely accused of an assassination attempt on the life of Governor Boggs of Missouri. Porter Rockwell had been kidnapped and taken to Missouri as Joseph Smith's accomplice. In order to obtain money to pay lawyer fees, the Prophet Joseph was lent $100 by a Brother Thomas Pomeroy, much to the chagrin of Thomas' sister, Katie, who doubted the money would ever be repaid. Despite lack of support from the family for his decision, Brother Pomeroy loaned Joseph Smith the money, receiving the promise from the Prophet that, "This shall be returned within three days, if I am alive." On a cold, rainy day late into the night, Brother Thomas arose to a knock at the door. It was the third day. There in the driving rain stood Joseph Smith. "Here Brother Thomas, is the money." A light was struck, and seated at the table he counted out the $100 in gold. He said, "Brother Thomas, I have been trying all day to raise this sum, for *my honor* was at stake. God bless you" (*Young Woman's Journal*, December 1906, p. 539; emphasis added).

We live in a wonderful time. The gospel is here in its fulness. The Lord needs you, the youth of Zion, to stand up for "truth and righteousness." The Ten Commandments are not outdated or ancient; it would be well for us to adopt and live them now in our lives. "Thou shalt not steal" and "Thou shalt not bear false witness" are still very powerful laws of honesty and integrity by which to live. President Hinckley, quoting ABC news reporter Ted Koppel said, "In its purest form, truth is not a polite tap on the shoulder. It is a howling reproach. What Moses brought down from Mount Sinai were *not* the Ten Suggestions" ("Our Solemn Responsibilities," *Ensign*, November 1991 p. 51).

We can all do a little better. We can lie less. We can study more and cheat less. We can strive more to think virtuous thoughts and express those thoughts, strengthening our integrity. We can check ourselves on unkind and needless gossip and rumor. We can repent and forgive more. For those of you troubled with dishonesty, keep working and striving to overcome this obstacle. Your efforts will be worth the struggle. For those of you who in your heart strive to be honest in thoughts, words, and actions (see Mosiah 4:30), I salute you. Keep taking a stand for truth and honesty. I bear you my solemn witness that "honesty *is* the best policy!"

***Gary R. Nelson** received his bachelor's degree in business education at Southern Utah University and master's degree in educational administration at Brigham Young University. He teaches seminary at Dixie High School in St. George, Utah. A popular youth and motivational speaker, he has been associated with EFY and Know Your Religion programs for many years. Gary is a former high school and collegiate football and tennis player and maintains an interest in all sports, especially Brigham Young University athletics. He has been a sportswriter for two local newspapers. In addition to writing and speaking, he enjoys making "animal imitations," singing, playing the guitar and piano, hunting, fishing, camping, bodysurfing, scuba diving, traveling, and spending time with his family. Gary and his wife, Christine, are the parents of seven children.*

20

Be a Builder, Not a Wrecker

Barbara Barrington Jones

Have you ever put on a pair of glasses with colored lenses? For instance, those yellow-tinted glasses that snow skiers wear to make the bumps and changes show up on a slope that would otherwise look flat and white. Suddenly everything looks different, more interesting, and often more beautiful.

You may have heard the term "looking at the world through rose-colored glasses." People use that phrase to mean that the person wearing rose-colored glasses sees the good in everything because everything looks rosy and warm.

I've often thought it would be nice if we could look at the world through Jesus-colored glasses. If we could look at the world through Jesus-colored glasses (let's call them "Son glasses"), we would be builders just like Christ wanted us to be for each other. But if we look at the world through Satan-colored glasses, we view the world the way he looks at it—negatively, critically, and judgmentally.

Kenneth Cope wrote a song called, "Backwords." No, that is not misspelled. "Backwords" are the damaging words spoken behind someone's back. The lyrics to his song go like this:

Whether carefully begun to scar a name,
Or recklessly continued without shame,
Self-approval is the underlying plan.
Fueled until the fire gets out of hand,
Catastrophe—crippling words behind the scenes,
Heartless talk that steals tomorrow's dreams.

Chorus

Who's gonna stop it? Who can,
Once it gets started spreading, threatening.
Has love become lost in the backwords path?

Now we pray for peace to keep us from the sword.
Then we turn and wound a brother with a word.
It's tragedy—blind to hypocrisy.
We're wanting love when we're love's enemy.

This road we take leads us to a bitter fate,
Where judgment's terror stares us in the face.
Who's gonna stop it, who then,
When justice gets started and we're not ready?
Regretting forever back words.
Who's gonna stop it? We can!
It's now or never.
Let's change forever,
And welcome love back to the forwards path.

How many times do we hear gossip and allow it to continue on because we love secrets? But secrets can become rumors which, in turn, become gossip. Wrong assumptions can spread and be used by Satan to wreck people's lives.

In one high school there was a girl who was always causing problems, always saying negative things, always gossiping. One day she could not wait to tell the entire school that she had seen the most popular boy and girl coming out of a motel at midnight. "Well, I actually didn't see them," she said to other students, "but my mom and dad were coming home from a party and saw them coming out of a motel."

You know how it is when someone tells you something like that. The gossip—the wrecking—begins. The truth was the young girl and boy had had car trouble and had gone to the motel to use the phone in the lobby.

To give another example, a girl was sitting in the waiting room at a doctor's office when a boy walked out. The girl was wearing her Satan-colored glasses and the boy was considered to be something of a nerd at school. When the girl heard the nurse say that the report was back and it was HIV-positive, she spread the gossip that this boy was HIV-positive. Because of this, the boy and his family found life so intolerable that they eventually had to move. However, the report had been regarding another patient, and the girl jumped to the wrong conclusion, wrecking the lives of some good, innocent people.

We choose to look at life through our own glasses. Which ones do you use? As we venture through life let us try to learn to wear our "Son glasses." Let us seek to build instead of tear down, to be a light instead of a judge. Instead of criticizing, look for the good. See what you can do to help the situation.

Stephen Covey, a nationally famous speaker and writer, tells of the time he got on a subway in a large city. There was a man in the same car with four little boys that were going wild. They were disrupting the whole subway car, running up and down the aisles. Finally Stephen Covey could stand it no longer. He approached the man and said, "Sir, pardon me, but I want you to know your children are disturbing everyone. Can't you control your children? Isn't there anything you can do?

The man looked up at him and said, "I'm sorry. I just came from the hospital where their mother died. I just don't quite know what to say to them right now. They've had such a shock. I don't want to be too strict. I'm sorry."

Brother Covey said that all of a sudden he felt very small. He had been looking at the situation through wrong-colored glasses. If he had Jesus-colored glasses on, he would not have said anything. His thought would have been, *I wonder what is wrong with that man. I wonder if there is anything I could do to help him.*

I'm sure you've heard your mother say, "If you can't say something nice, don't say anything at all." It's good advice. Build others up and make them feel good about themselves. Be helpful in a situation, and you will end up being the true winner.

You may be familiar with some of the different books written by people who have had near-death experiences. I'm not sure I believe everything people have said about their experiences, but one woman said something that made me think. She said that when she died and went into the next life, she was allowed to look back at the world. Looking back, she saw that many people were surrounded by an "aura," which means a distinctive atmosphere around a person or object. Some people had a black aura around them, and they produced and spread negative actions and thoughts and in return received the same. Other people had a white aura around them. They gave out good to others and received good in return. The more goodness they gave, the more goodness they received. Their light was beautiful, bright, and uplifting.

That is how I want you to be—a person with a white aura. Don't be a judge. Be a light to the world! Don't be a gossip. Don't spread rumors or say cutting remarks about others.

I'd like to tell you about a girl I'll call Amber. She said, "I have been made fun of all my life. At school, peers would say, 'Oh, here comes thunder thighs,' or 'Fat Albert's wife is coming.' These things hurt me deeply. I have never had a best friend or a really close friend. I normally had lunch by myself and did nothing on the weekends. I was nearly always by myself.

"The final straw was when my family started making rude comments. My brothers and sisters and father would say, 'Don't you care about yourself?' But the most hurtful thing of all was when my mother said, 'Because of the way you look and the way you act, you will never have a boyfriend or get married.' I went to school that day and cried for two hours in the health office. I then decided that there was no purpose to my life since I had no one to talk to about the way I felt. I decided to take my life."

Fortunately, Amber was able to find healing before she could carry out her decision. She wrote me later to tell me how she had attended a youth camp I taught called "A Look At You," held on the campus of Brigham Young University. I talked to the young women who attended this camp about letting the inner beauty each person has show on the outside. Amber learned that depending on the Lord, studying the scriptures, pondering, fasting, and praying brought her a new best friend, one that would never hurt her—Jesus Christ. This literally saved her life. Amber also realized that she has a special mission to complete on this earth.

With the confidence this knowledge gave her, Amber found the courage to talk with her family about her feelings. She was able to forgive her mother and everyone who had hurt her in the past.

When I was in high school, I was very shy. I literally had only one friend, Lynne Hartman, who was tall and shy like me. Then Rick, who was short and introverted, entered our high school. Rick had attended high school at a Catholic seminary until the last six weeks of his senior year when he came to our high school. I felt sorry for Rick because he didn't know anyone and didn't fit in. I started talking to him on the bus and found I could talk to him because he was even more shy than I was. I became his friend and we talked every day about all kinds of things.

On the last day of school, I boarded the bus with my yearbook in hand. When Rick sat down next to me, I asked him if he would sign my yearbook. I made sure he didn't see that my friend, Lynne, was the only one who had signed my book. When he finished writing, he closed it and handed it back to me. I was in a rush to make it to a ballet class, and it wasn't until later that night that I opened my yearbook to see what Rick had written. This is what I read:

> Dear Barb,
>
> Your strength of character, your marvelous personality, your exceptional beauty have been an inspiration to me in many ways. I thank you for the most important thing, the importance of religion outside of the seminary. One of the things I like best about you is I've never heard you say anything bad about anyone. You're always trying to help everyone. You've been like a sister to me and a great friend. You're a wonderful person to know and you couldn't be more

perfect. Here's to our short friendship. May it never end. Always willing to help you.

Love, Rick, the ex-seminarian

I think that short paragraph changed my life. I must have read what he wrote a thousand times. He built me up and made me feel good about myself.

My mom is another example of someone who builds people up. When I was fourteen, my mother was a volunteer in a hospital. One day she decided to make certain patients "the hospital queen" for a day. She made a paper crown decorated with glitter, and a white banner out of some ribbon. She created a bouquet out of some artificial roses she had in the garage and made a poster that said, "Hospital Queen." To top it all off, she made me her "official photographer."

Every week I had to go with my mother into somebody's room and make the presentation to someone we didn't even know. I thought it was the dumbest thing, and I was completely humiliated.

Then one day, I heard a woman talking on a pay telephone about it. She was saying, "You'll never believe this, but Mother was chosen hospital queen. Out of all the people in this hospital, she was chosen the queen! She had a crown, a banner, and a bouquet. And we even have a picture of it. Yes, I'll send you a copy. I'll make thirty copies to send to all the family and her friends." I saw then that people actually enjoyed what my mother was doing, and that people liked how it made them feel.

My mother did those kinds of things her whole life. When someone she knew had their picture in the newspaper, she would cut it out and laminate it on a piece of paper decorated with flowers. She'd write "Congratulations!" on it and send it to them. Just the other day a woman told me how my mother, even though she's in a rest home today suffering from Alzheimer's, gave this woman an award, a few words written on a scrap of paper in tiny handwriting. Even now, when there is hardly anything left of her, my mother is still a builder.

Be a builder. Be a light to the world. Remember to wear your "Son glasses." Tell a young girl she has beautiful eyes. Tell your dad he's wonderful. Write five thank-you notes every Sunday. Look for the good in every person and every situation. Let your white light be contagious. "Let your light so shine before men that they may see your good works and glorify your Father which is in heaven" (Matthew 5:16). When you build people up, you become a winner yourself.

When Christ was teaching his disciples, he told them that the greatest commandment was to love their Lord and God. The second commandment, no less important, is to "love one another; as I have loved you" (John 13:34).

I know that God lives. I know that Jesus is the Christ. I know there is power in his name. Call upon him and look to his light to guide you along the journey back home.

An international image consultant, author, lecturer, and fashion designer, ***Barbara Barrington Jones*** *is a former professional classical ballet dancer. She is also a member of the President's Roundtable Advisory Board for Brigham Young University-Hawaii and directs a summer program for women. Barbara and her husband, Hal, have two children, each of whom has served a mission and married in the temple.*

21

Birthright Blessings

R. Scott Simmons

In the Old Testament there is an interesting story about a young man named Esau. Esau was Isaac's son and the brother of Jacob. This is the same Jacob who had his name changed to Israel and became the father of the Israelite nation. Do you have your Bible? If you don't, go get it right now, and while you're at it, grab your triple combination, too. *Wait.* You will also need a red pencil or something to mark with. This will make a lot more sense to you if you can see it in the scriptures.

Okay, are you ready? Open your Bible to the dictionary and look up the word "birthright." You will find it on page 625. Now read the entry. Do you understand what a birthright is? It is, simply, those special rights and privileges given to the firstborn son so that he could take care of the family. If this son kept his birthright, he received special blessings. The Savior has the birthright for us. He is the firstborn son and he has been given special rights and privileges so that he can bless us.

You and I have also been given a birthright. We have been given special rights and privileges that allow us to bless the lives of those around us. If we keep our birthright we will receive great blessings. Sometimes we don't realize what a great blessing this birthright is, so we sell it for something that gives us more immediate satisfaction without all the responsibility. This is what Esau did. Were you wondering if we would ever get back to him? Now turn to Genesis 25:29-34 and read. As you read, ask yourself these questions: (1) What did Esau sell his birthright for? and (2) How did Esau feel about his birthright?

Well, what do you think? Pull out your journal and write down your answers. Also, write down how you think this applies to you. Some questions you might ask yourself are: Do I know what my birthright is? Have I kept my birthright or have I sold it? What are the special blessings and privileges I have received with my birthright? Okay, write.

You may have felt as you read that this was a pretty sneaky thing for Jacob to do. After all, here is his brother about to die from hunger, and Jacob cons him out of his birthright. But this wasn't the case at all. It says in verse 34 that Esau "despised his birthright." In other words, Esau couldn't have cared less for his birthright. To him it just meant extra responsibility without immediate blessings. He wasn't dying, he was simply hungry. He wanted food now and was willing to sell his birthright to get it. That's how much his birthright meant to him—a bowl of soup. How much does your birthright mean to you? Take a minute and write your answer to that question in your journal.

Think about how many of us do the very same thing? Because we do not realize how much our birthright is worth, we sell it for something more immediate. For example, one of the blessings of your birthright is to be married in the temple. This means that if you live righteously you can be with the one you love, not just for time, but for eternity. Yet some people sell that blessing for more immediate satisfaction. They break the law of chastity and sell their birthright. You can get your birthright back, but the process is difficult. It is better not to sell it in the first place.

At April conference in 1986, President Benson gave a talk titled "To the Youth of the Noble Birthright." In his talk he outlined seven things that you and I could do to keep from selling our birthright. Let's take a look at what he said.

STAY CLOSE TO YOUR FAMILIES

President Benson said, "I counsel each of you to draw close to your own mother. Respect her. Honor her. Receive your mother's counsel as she loves and instructs you in righteousness. And honor and obey your father as he stands as the head of the home, emulating his manly qualities. . . . The family unit is forever, and you should do everything in your power to strengthen that unit. In your own family, encourage family home evenings and be an active participant. Encourage family prayer and be on your knees with your family in that sacred circle. Do your part to develop real family unity and solidarity. In such homes, there is no generation gap. Your most important friendships should be with your own brothers and sisters and with your father and mother. Love your family. Be loyal to them. Have a genuine concern for your brothers and sisters. Help carry their load so you can say, like the lyrics of that song, 'He ain't heavy; he's my brother.' Remember, the family is one of God's greatest fortresses against the evils of our day. Help keep your family strong and close and worthy of our Father in Heaven's blessings. As you do, you will receive faith and strength which will bless your lives forever."

How are you doing? Are you staying close to your family? What thoughts and impressions came to your mind and heart as you read President Benson's advice? Take a minute and write down how you felt in your journal. If you feel like there are some specific things you need to do, you may want to kneel down and ask your Father in Heaven to help you do those things.

READ AND PONDER THE SCRIPTURES DAILY, ESPECIALLY THE BOOK OF MORMON

"The Book of Mormon will change your life," President Benson said. "It will fortify you against the evils of our day. It will bring a spirituality into your life that no other book will. It will be the most important book you will read in preparation for a mission and for life. A young [person] who knows and loves the Book of Mormon, who has read it several times, who has an abiding testimony of its truthfulness, and who applies its teachings will be able to stand against the wiles of the devil and will be a mighty tool in the hands of the Lord."

How did you feel as you read President Benson's advice? What did you feel impressed to do? Stop and write those impressions in your journal. You may also pray and ask for help to do what you need to do.

One young woman I know felt like she needed to read her Book of Mormon more. The best time for her to read was during lunch. So she did, every day. Now she was the only member of the church in her high school, and she was also the student-body president. She told me that when she first started to read, some of the other students made fun of her, but after a while they began reading with her. What happened to change them? One day one of her friends asked her what she was reading. When she told her "the scriptures," her friend said she liked to read the scriptures, too. This young woman told her friend these were different scriptures. These scriptures contained an account of the Savior's visit to the American continent. When her friend asked where she could get a copy of this book, she immediately pulled a blue paperback copy out of her backpack and handed it to her. School had only been going for two weeks and this young woman had six of her nonmember friends reading the Book of Mormon with her, every day, at lunch. That is the power of the Book of Mormon.

OBTAIN YOUR PATRIARCHAL BLESSING AND STUDY IT OFTEN

President Benson said, "Receive a patriarchal blessing. Study it carefully and regard it as personal scripture to you—-for that is what it is. A patriarchal blessing is the inspired and prophetic statement of your life's mission together with blessings, cautions, and admonitions as the patriarch may be prompted to give. Young [people], receive your patriarchal blessing under the influence of fasting and prayer, and then read it regularly that you may know God's will for you."

Now go ahead and write down your impressions. You may feel you need to get your patriarchal blessing. Or, if you have already received it, you may feel you need to study your blessing. Whatever you feel, write it down.

Are you beginning to get the idea? I am not only teaching you about your birthright, I am teaching you how to read and study your scriptures and the words of the prophets so they will bring you closer to the Savior and his Atonement. If you will honestly answer the questions and pray for help to do what you feel you need to do, you will feel your Father in Heaven's love for you.

ATTEND ALL YOUR CHURCH MEETINGS

Referring to "the importance of attending all of your Church meetings," President Benson said, *"Faithful attendance at Church meetings brings blessings you can receive in no other way."*

Did you catch that? "Faithful attendance at Church meetings brings blessings you can receive in no other way." Take a minute and think about that. What kind of blessings do you think he is talking about? How do you think we receive those blessings?

President Benson went on to say, "Attend your sacrament meeting every Sunday. Listen carefully to the messages. Pray for the spirit of understanding and testimony. Be worthy to prepare and bless and pass the sacrament. Come to the sacrament table with clean hands and a pure heart. Attend your Sunday School classes every Sunday. Listen carefully to the lesson and participate in class discussions. Gospel scholarship and an increase in testimony will result. Regularly attend seminary and be a seminary graduate. Seminary instruction is one of the most significant spiritual experiences a young [person] can have."

In the Old Testament we read another example where someone foolishly sold his birthright. Before you record your impressions this time pull your Bible out again and turn to 2 Samuel 11. It is on page 439 in your Bible. David was able to slay the giant Goliath because of his faithfulness, but later he committed adultery, and even murder. Because of this he lost all he had.

I want you to read verses 1-4 and see if you can tell where David's downward slide began. Okay, read.

What do you think? Was his first step toward sin when he looked at Bathsheba? Or was it when he sent for her? Or was it even before that? Let me give you a little help. Read verse 1 again. Where was David supposed to be? In verse 1 we read that David was supposed to be at the battle, but instead he had tarried at Jerusalem. So, if David had just been where he should have been, he might not have sinned.

What does this story teach you about attending your Church

meetings? Take a few minutes and record your impressions. You may want to mark those verses in your Bible and even write a note out in the margin like, "Always be where you are supposed to be."

Well, we're more than halfway through President Benson's steps. How are you doing? Are you thinking that it's taking a long time to get through this article this way? If you are, feel free to stop. Read a little each day, if that helps. If you're doing okay, go on.

BE A MISSIONARY

Next President Benson said, "May I now speak with you about missionary service in the kingdom. I feel very deeply about this. I pray that you will understand the yearnings of my heart. The Prophet Joseph Smith said, 'After all that has been said, [our] greatest and most important duty is to preach the Gospel' *(Teachings of the Prophet Joseph Smith*, sel. Joseph Fielding Smith [Salt Lake City: Deseret Book Co., 1938], p. 113). You can do nothing more important."

Before you write your impressions, open your Book of Mormon to Alma 17. This is the story of the sons of Mosiah and their mission to the Lamanites. Carefully read chapters 17-20 and look for the things that Ammon did to be a great missionary. When you find something, highlight it. Not the whole verse, just what he did. When you are finished, make a list of these things in your journal. Okay, read.

How was it? Did you find some wonderful things? As you record your impressions, think about how you can do some of the things Ammon did, so that you will be a great missionary.

STAY CLEAN

President Benson gave the following counsel: "Always live a clean life. We want morally clean young men in the mission field. We want you to live the clean life all of your life. We want the morally clean life to be your way of life. Yes, one can repent of moral transgression. The miracle of forgiveness is real, and true repentance is accepted of the Lord. But it is not pleasing to the Lord prior to a mission, or at any time, to sow one's wild oats, to engage in sexual transgression of any nature, and then to expect that planned confession and quick repentance will satisfy the Lord. President Kimball was emphatic on this point. In his marvelous book *The Miracle of Forgiveness*, he stated: 'That man who resists temptation and lives without sin is far better off than the man who has fallen, no matter how repentant the latter may be. . . . How much better it is never to have committed sin!'" (Salt Lake City: Bookcraft, 1969, p. 357).

How are you doing? If you are feeling like you need to change, do it. I testify that your Father in Heaven loves you and that you have a Savior who paid for your sins. I testify that the process of repentance is real and that you can be fully clean. Go see your bishop if you need to. He loves you. If you're not sure if you need to see your bishop, ask him. He can tell you what sins you will need his help in overcoming and what sins you can overcome without him. If you are afraid to go see your bishop, talk to your parents first or a leader, or teacher. They can help give you the courage to see him. Once again I testify that you are loved and you can be clean. If you are clean, stay that way. Keep your birthright safe.

FILL YOUR LIFE WITH LIGHT

President Benson asks us to remember Alma's words to his son Corianton: "'Forsake your sins, and go no more after the lusts of your eyes' (Alma 39:9). 'The lusts of your eyes.' In our day, what does that expression mean? Movies, television programs, and video recordings that are both suggestive and lewd. Magazines and books that are obscene and pornographic. We counsel you . . . not to pollute your minds with such degrading matter, for the mind through which this filth passes is never the same afterwards. Don't see R-rated movies or vulgar videos or participate in any entertainment that is immoral, suggestive, or pornographic. Don't listen to music that is degrading. Remember Elder Boyd K. Packer's statement: 'Music, once . . . innocent, now is often used for wicked purposes. . . . In our day music itself has been corrupted. Music can, by its tempo, by its beat, by its intensity [and I would add by its lyrics], dull the spiritual sensitivity of men. . . . Elder Packer goes on to say, 'You cannot afford to fill your mind with the unworthy hard music of our day' (in *Conference Report*, October, 1973, pp. 21, 25; or *Ensign*, January, 1974, pp. 25, 28). Instead, we encourage you to listen to uplifting music, both popular and classical, that builds the Spirit. Learn some favorite hymns from our new hymnbook that build faith and spirituality. Attend dances where the music and the lighting and the dance movements are conducive to the Spirit. Watch those shows and entertainment that lift the spirit and promote clean thoughts and actions. Read books and magazines that do the same."

All right, you know what to do. Write down your impressions. Remember, if you will ask your Father in Heaven he will help you. Remember what Nephi told his father. Open your Book of Mormon and read 1 Nephi 3:7. That is quite a promise. The Lord will not ask us to do anything without helping us do it. Ask.

Let's review the seven things you can do to keep your birthright blessings safe:

1. Stay close to your family.
2. Read and ponder the scriptures daily.
3. Get and read your patriarchal blessing often.
4. Attend your Church meetings.
5. Be a missionary.
6. Stay clean.
7. Fill your life with light.

I testify that if you will do the things President Benson has counseled us to do, your birthright blessings will be safe and you will enjoy great peace and happiness in this life. I testify that your Father in Heaven will help you do these things and that if you will always do these things you will receive the greatest blessing of your birthright—eternal life. God lives. Jesus is the Christ. The scriptures are true. We have a prophet on the earth today who leads the Savior's church, even The Church of Jesus Christ of Latter-day Saints. In the name of Jesus Christ. Amen.

***R. Scott Simmons** was born and raised in Salt Lake City, Utah. He served a mission in Cleveland, Ohio, and graduated from Brigham Young University. He is a part-time instructor of ancient scripture at Brigham Young University. He enjoys hunting, fishing, and camping. He and his wife, Nancy, live in Highland, Utah.*

22

My Friend Jesus Suffered for My Pain

Kory Kunz

During my thirty-three years of mortal existence I have come to the conclusion that pain is painful. I have also decided that there is a purpose for that pain. When your body feels pain, it tells you that something is wrong. At times, physical pain can be so intense and severe that one must have medical attention in order to stay alive.

There is another kind of pain called spiritual pain. This kind of pain also has a purpose. It tells you that something is spiritually wrong and that spiritual attention is needed to insure that your spirit will not be damaged. If you listen to spiritual pain, it is telling you that there is a need to repent.

When I was younger, there was a popular children's game called "Swing on Grandpa's Gate." All one needed to play this game was a gate (preferably a grandpa's) and one other person. One person sat on the gate and the other opened the gate until the spring was very tight. Then the person holding the gate let go. For young children this activity was nearly as exciting as an amusement park ride.

Many years ago my brother and I were playing "Swing on Grandpa's Gate." It was my turn to sit on the gate, and my brother did his duty by opening the gate and letting go. The force of gravity threw my skinny, little body off the gate, and I landed on the ground head first. That was painful enough by itself. What made it even worse was that I landed on Grandpa's garden rake. As I stood up, my brother was shocked to see the rake stuck in my head. We pulled the rake out and he hurried me into my grandpa's house.

Inside, my mother took over. I was expecting to be comforted and soothed, but a mother's tender comfort was not what I received. Instead, she parted my hair, opened the wound up, and cleaned it out!

"Why did you do that?" I asked, in pain.

"I have to clean it or it will not heal," she responded. Right then and there I decided that mothers were mean and that they must enjoy seeing their children suffer! I knew I would be glad when I no longer had to have a mother around to cause me pain in my time of need.

Years went by and I got married. A couple years ago I had another "Grandpa's Gate" incident. I was playing church basketball and put my head in the wrong place: I put it in the path of a moving elbow. The elbow struck me on the head and blood began to pour out. I called "time out" to stop the game and I ran to the rest room. My teammates followed, and even though I needed stitches they told me a Band-Aid™ would suffice. With the Band-Aid™ on, my head continued to bleed until the moment I walked in my front door. Inside, my wife took over. I wanted to be comforted and soothed, but instead she opened the wound and cleaned it out.

"Why did you have to do that?" I whined.

In response she said, "I have to clean it or it won't heal . . . you big baby." Right then and there I decided that wives were just as mean as mothers, and that they enjoyed seeing their husbands suffer!

We all sin and all sins are spiritual wounds. If left alone, these wounds will become infected with guilt and despair. The infection can spread in an attempt to weaken and kill the spirit. Repentance is like opening up and cleaning out the wound. Like medication on an open wound, it may even sting a little. What we want is to be comforted and soothed. However, if the wound is not cleansed, we find no comfort. The spirit cannot be healed without this important step.

Our Savior can take over and help us open our wounds to him. He has already felt the pain of our wounds and wants so very much to cleanse us and take away our sins.

Our decision to repent and the process that follows may be a painful one. However, true repentance brings complete joy and saves us from additional pain that comes later in life and that will come on the Judgement Day.

Have you ever had the dream where you go to school in your underwear? I hope I'm not the only one who has had this embarrassing dream. The amazing thing about that dream for me is that no one in my dream tells me of my poor choice in apparel. My brothers and sisters don't tell me at the breakfast table. My dad doesn't tell me while I'm brushing my teeth. My mom doesn't stop me as I say goodbye and walk out the front door. And most amazingly, the bus driver doesn't stop me from coming on the bus. Surely there must be a rule that no "underwear people" can ride the bus. What a pleasure it is when I awake to find it was only a dream.

As weird as it may seem, that dream could become a reality at the judgment bar. Jacob talked about how we will feel on the Judgment Day if we have chosen not to repent. "Wherefore, we shall have a perfect knowledge of all our guilt, and our uncleanness, and *our nakedness*" (2 Nephi 9:14; emphasis added). The embarrassment that we might have felt during that dream will pale in comparison to the feeling we will have at that moment. We will not be literally naked, but rather, because our Savior knows everything about us, we will feel completely exposed to him. He will see all our sins.

But there is a good side to that same special event. If we choose to repent, we will feel comfortably clothed at the judgment. "And the righteous shall have a perfect knowledge of their enjoyment, and their righteousness, *being clothed with purity,* yea, even with the robe of righteousness" (2 Nephi 9:14; emphasis added). What a wonderful feeling that will be to wear the robe of righteousness, to stand before the Savior, open to his all-searching and loving eyes, and to be clothed with purity. The decision to repent *now* will determine whether we will feel naked or clothed at the Judgment.

Choosing to feel the pains of repentance now will also keep us from feeling a great deal more pain later. The Savior tells us that if we choose not to repent in this life, we will feel the pains of the atonement in the next. "Therefore I command you to repent—repent, lest I smite you by the rod of my mouth, and by my wrath, and by my anger, and your sufferings be sore—how sore you know not, how exquisite you know not, yea, how hard to bear you know not" (D&C 19:15).

The Savior so dearly wants us to repent. If we choose not to repent, it appears that he will be angry with us—not because he *does not* love us, but because he *does* love us. He loves us enough that he suffered the pains of our sins before we were even born. He also warns us repeatedly that we will suffer if we choose not to repent. We cannot even imagine how painful our suffering will be if we don't take advantage of repentance. How does he know how that pain will feel? Because he felt that pain.

"For behold, I, God, have suffered these things for all, that they might not suffer if they would repent; but if they would not repent they must suffer even as I; which suffering caused myself, even God, the greatest of all, to tremble because of pain, and to bleed at every pore, and to suffer both body and spirit—and would that I might not drink the bitter cup, and shrink" (D&C 19:16-18). If we choose to repent in this life, his atonement pays for those sins. But if we choose not to repent, *we* will have to atone for our own sins before the judgment bar. I hope that we do not let one drop of the Savior's blood fall in vain.

I want to take you on an imaginary trip with me. Imagine that while you are laying in your bed tonight you begin to feel sick to your stomach. A sharp pain stabs you deep inside and you begin to vomit. This continues for hours. After you tell your parents of your illness, they decide to take you to the hospital. You enter the emergency room and the doctor on duty examines you.

"You have appendicitis," the doctor says. "Your appendix is inflamed, and if it is not removed within the hour, it will rupture, spreading an infectious poison throughout your body."

"Okay," you think to yourself, "let's start the operation. What are we waiting for?"

At your look of impatience, the doctor continues, "But there is one problem. The hospital is out of anesthetic."

"Get it from another hospital," you exclaim.

"As a matter of fact," the doctor replies, "the entire state is out of anesthetic."

"Get it from another state," you plead.

"Not only are all the states out of anesthetic, but there is not one drop in the entire world," the doctor apologizes. "You'll have to make a decision. You can either choose to lie down on the operating table and allow me to remove your appendix without any anesthetic, or you will die."

As you sadly consider your situation, a man walks into the room. You have never seen this man before. He turns to you and with a smile says, "I can help you."

You shake your head. "Unless you have some anesthetic in your pocket," you say, "you cannot help me."

"But I *can* help you," he continues, "if you will only believe. My appendix is perfect, without spot or blemish. There has never been nor ever will be an appendix like mine. I will lie down on the operating table for you and allow the doctor to remove my perfect appendix without any anesthetic. That way I will feel your pain for you. If you accept this trade, you can have your diseased appendix removed through me." As he speaks, he looks into your eyes, into your very soul and asks, "Will you let me do this for you?" You nod your head in wonder, and he answers your unspoken question, "I will do this because I love you."

"Thank you," you say through your tears. "I believe."

We do have a spiritual disease. It is called sin. It can only be removed when we repent and let the Savior's atonement into our lives. He is the only one who knew no sin. He is without spot or blemish. The perfect sacrifice. But it is our choice. He cannot and will not force us to repent and be healed. Imagine his sadness when we choose to continue in our ways of sin. When we choose not to use the divine, healing help that the atonement can bring, we turn away from him. On the other hand, imagine his joy when we choose to repent and come unto him.

There are certain sins that require another person's help to clean out our spiritual wounds—someone who is to assist the Savior in this cleansing process. That person is your bishop. Sins for which you need to see your bishop would include most moral transgressions and Word of Wisdom problems. You may be afraid to go to your bishop. You may fear that he will not understand you and your problem, or that he will look at you differently after you confess your sin to him.

But I can promise you, your bishop loves you. Remember how I felt when my mom and my wife cleaned out my wounds? At first I was mad, but in time I came to realize it was for my own good. Your bishop has no desire to cause you pain, but it is his job to clean out the wound so that the infection does not spread. The Savior, through your bishop's help, can not only clean out your spiritual wounds but can completely remove the scars. "Behold, he who has repented of his sins, the same is forgiven, and I, the Lord, remember them no more" (D&C 58:42).

Sin produces thoughts of loneliness and despair. Jesus Christ's atonement is the only way for us to be relieved of these feelings. We cannot do it alone. We need his divine help. One of the songs that I have written is about the atonement and the way that our Savior can help us.

Who can I tell? Who'll understand the way I feel?
I'm all alone; there's no one that I can tell.
On my knees, I feel the pain, I pray to feel His love again.
Only a friend forgives me time and time again.

As I pray, He is by my side. He calls my name. I wonder why
For me this man would suffer, bleed, and die.
Suddenly, I see Him fall and on His knees He suffers all.
He looks at me and I see a teardrop fall.

He is my friend. He suffers for my pain.
He gives when I've nothing left to pay.
And He lives. He cries when I lose my way.
He loves me in my darkest day.
When no one is my friend, He is.

The Savior is more than a friend. He is the only one who can take our sins upon himself to relieve our pain. He took our pain when we were unable to pay for our sins. The prophet Alma tells us, "Now the Spirit knoweth all things; nevertheless the Son of God suffereth according to the flesh that he might take upon him the sins of his people, that he might blot out their transgressions according to the power of his deliverance; and now behold, this is the testimony which is in me" (Alma 7:13).

This is the testimony which is in me, that Christ does live. I know that he loves each of us more than we will ever know. And because of that love, our sins can be removed if we will repent.

Kory Kunz *teaches seminary in Vernal, Utah. He holds a bachelor's degree in communications from the University of Utah and served a Spanish-speaking mission in Tampa, Florida. Kory is a singer and songwriter and enjoys all kinds of sports. Kory currently serves as ward mission leader. Kory and his wife, Lynette, have four children.*

23

Making Decisions That Last

Art E. Berg

Several months ago I received a letter from someone who had read one of my books. The return address on the outside of the label revealed that the writer was in prison in Texas. Once an active, faithful member of the Church, this young man had made some bad choices over a period of time that ultimately lead to his incarceration. Now he was distraught and repentant, and wanted to change.

However, a prison environment is not exactly an ideal place to find the moral support necessary for making a lasting change. In a tone of desperation, the young man asked me if I could help him. I could feel his pain through the pages as I read each sentence over and over again. He asked, "How can I stick to my resolve? How can I change? How do I continue to progress even within these prison walls?"

Wanting to help, I wrote him a letter. Unfortunately, that letter was returned to me several weeks later unopened with the words imprinted on the envelope, "RETURN TO SENDER. ADDRESSEE UNKNOWN." For weeks I searched for a proper address for my new friend, only to be disappointed at every turn.

I would like to share with you the letter I wrote him, with the hope that one day this young man will come across these words. In the meantime, I hope it makes as profound a difference for you as it has for me.

Dear Jeremy,

Thank you for your letter. I was honored that you thought enough of my book to write me. I am sorry that it has taken me so long to respond. However, your letter has caused me to spend a lot of time reflecting on your question, "How do I continue to progress?"

I have often struggled in my own life with "doing the right thing." I have also battled with maintaining my spiritual resolve as you are now doing. I don't think we are in poor company. The Apostle Paul sadly proclaimed, "But I am carnal, sold under sin. . . . For the good that I would I do not: but the evil which I would not, that I do. . . . Oh wretched man that I am!" (Romans 7: 14, 19, 24). Even the faithful Nephi felt compelled to say, "Oh wretched man that I am! Yea, my heart sorroweth because of my flesh; my soul grieveth because of mine iniquities. I am encompassed about, because of the temptations and the sins which do so easily beset me. And when I desire to rejoice, my heart groaneth because of my sins" (2 Nephi 4: 17-19). Universally, good men everywhere have fought a war between their desires to do good and their nature to do evil.

In my own fight to win over the forces of evil, I have looked to the scriptures to uncover ideas and insights to strengthen my own resolve. One of the greatest examples I have discovered is found in Alma 24. You may recall that a group of the Lamanites had been converted to the gospel through the teachings of the missionary, Ammon. Their spiritual rebirth was so strong that they entered into a covenant with the Lord to never take up arms again against their brethren. This was quite a commitment. They basically decided that they would be willing to die before shedding other's blood again—even in their own defense! I'm not so sure my resolve would have been as strong as theirs. I might have committed to an easier version of their covenant. For example, I might have sworn an oath to never take up arms as long as my enemies didn't come against me. Or maybe I would have committed to never take up arms as long as my wife and children were not in danger. Or perhaps I would have decided to not take up arms, but I would certainly run from any potentially hostile encounter with my enemies.

The people of Ammon had a different resolve. Their commitment was firm and unyielding. There were no conditions made on their covenant. The scriptures record, "Now when the people [of Ammon] saw that [the Lamanites] were coming against them they went out to meet them, and prostrated themselves before them to the earth, and began to call on the name of the Lord; and thus they were in this attitude when the Lamanites began to fall upon them, and began to slay them with the sword. And thus without meeting any resistance, they did slay a thousand and five of them" (Alma 24:21-22). Wow! How can I develop that kind of resolve? What more could I do if I could make and keep commitments with that kind of confidence and determination? How would it change my spiritual life, my exercise routines, my study habits, my relationships, and my integrity?

With further study, I noticed that the scriptures leave some clues as to how to duplicate that kind of resolve in my own life, regardless of whether it involves spiritual or temporal matters. The formula I discovered was found in the following words:

> And now, my brethren, if our brethren seek to destroy us, behold, we will hide away our swords, yea, even we will bury them deep in the earth, that they may be kept bright, as a testimony that we have never used them, at the last day; and if our brethren destroy us, behold, we shall go to our God and shall be saved.
>
> And now it came to pass that when the king had made an end of these sayings, and all the people were assembled together, they took their swords, and all the weapons which were used for the shedding of man's blood, and they did bury them up deep in the earth.
>
> And this they did, it being their view a testimony to God, and also to men, that they never would use weapons again for the shedding of man's blood; and this they did, vouching and covenanting with God, that rather than shed the blood of their brethren they would give up their own

> lives; and rather than take away from a brother they would give unto him; and rather than spend their days in idleness they would labor abundantly with their hands. And thus we see that, when these Lamanites were brought to believe and to know the truth, they were firm, and would suffer even unto death rather than commit sin; and thus we see that they buried their weapons of . . . war, for peace." (Alma 24:16-19)

The people of Ammon did several things specifically that had a significant impact on the firmness of their resolve and the strength of their covenant:

1. They buried their swords and all weapons of war.

They didn't just put their weapons away in a closet, but the scriptures say that they did "hide away" and "bury them deep in the earth." I think we would be wise if we "buried deep" some physical temptations to return to our old habits. For the smoker it may mean to throw away ashtrays, packs of cigarettes, matches, and all the evidence of their lifestyle. For those struggling with their weight, it may mean to discard all foods which do not promote a healthy body. For those addicted to pornography, it means to remove all magazines, movies, books, and other sources of sensual stimulation from our work and homes. To bury these things "deep" means that we make access to them extremely difficult if not impossible. Too often we only discard of these things in shallow and temporary ways "just in case" we change our mind. This does not promote firm resolve.

2. They thought through the consequences of their decision in advance. They counted the cost of their covenant and settled on the ultimate price they were willing to pay.

How many times do we make commitments without really thinking through all that will be required of us to successfully complete them. We need to measure the cost in terms of time, resources, money, and people. We should consider the obstacles which will inevitably present themselves to us along the path. Ammon's people knew the price of their covenant could require everything they had when they stated, "and if our brethren destroy us, behold, we shall go to our God and shall be saved."

3. Unite yourself with other people who have made similar commitments.

The decision to not defend themselves was not made alone. The account from the scriptures says, "and all the people were assembled together." They were not only assembled together physically, but also spiritually and emotionally. They were of like mind, spirit, and heart. We too should assemble ourselves with others who support our decisions. We should hang around people who understand where we are going and are committed to helping us along the way. There is strength in numbers.

4. Know why you want to do something.

It's not enough to just know *what* you want to do, but also *why* you want to do it. If the *why* is strong enough, the *how* will usually take care of itself. Why is it important to change your behavior? Why do you want to live with God again? Why do you want to serve other people? Why would you rather follow Christ than Satan? Why? The people of Ammon knew why they wanted to enter into their covenant: "And this they did, it being their view a testimony to God." Other than as a testimony, they also were willing to bury "their weapons of . . . war, for peace." The stronger and more clear the *why*, the longer lasting the resolve.

5. Replace poor habits with better ones.

It's not enough just to stop doing something bad. The commitment will last substantially longer if we replace it with something positive and good. If you are going to give up pornography, replace it with a library of good, wholesome books. If you are going to give up smoking, replace it with a plan for exercise and better eating habits. If you want to clean up your language, replace it with increased service and expressions of gratitude to others. In the experience of the people of Ammon, they decided "that rather than shed the blood of their brethren they would give up their own lives; and rather than take away from a brother they would give unto him; and rather than spend their days in idleness they would labor abundantly with their hands."

Don't just give up old behavior that is bad. Decide what you will do right. Ask yourself, what would you rather do? What will you do instead of what you have been doing?

The scriptures make wonderful patterns to follow. While we all struggle with staying on course when it comes to spiritual matters, we can certainly strengthen our resolve—even to the extent that we become as Ammon's people when it states that they "were firm, and would suffer even unto death rather than commit sin." With that kind of discipline, all things become possible.

I empathize with your struggle. Don't give up. Follow the scriptures. Strengthen your resolve. And may God bless you always.

Art E. Berg *is a businessman and president of Invictus Communications, Inc. A professional speaker, he has written two books,* Some Miracles Take Time *and* Finding Peace in Troubled Waters. *He is a former early-morning seminary teacher and currently serves as a gospel doctrine instructor. Art enjoys wheelchair racing, parasailing, boating, and traveling. He and his wife, Dallas, have two children and make their home in Highland, Utah.*